日本語版・英語版 合本

ヒロシマの宿命を使命にかえて

原爆の語り部として生きる

竹岡智佐子

サンロータス研究所

撮影：木下清隆（2014 年）

娘・東野真里子　　　著 者　　　孫娘・東野絵美

講演中の著者（2009年5月30日）

國貞リョウ（1903〜1967）

この写真は、国立広島原爆死没者追悼平和祈念館地下2階の
遺影コーナーに登録され永久保存されている

＜写真説明文に「被爆時年齢　42歳　**被爆場所**　広島市船入
病院（広島市舟入病院）広島市舟入幸町（現在の広島市中区
舟入幸町）　**被爆時住所**　広島市己斐町上町区209－7　**被爆
時職業**　医療従事者［第2総軍第15方面軍広島第1陸軍病
院　婦長］」と記されている＞

母、竹岡智佐子は令和2年（2020年）12月31日に広島市安佐南区のメリィホスピタル（医療法人社団八千代会）で永眠しました。その病院で母は、折にふれ平和の大切さを語り、筆記して遺した原稿がありますので、そこでの母の写真とともに、ここに掲載いたします。（なお、2021年1月26日　広島ホームテレビで母の特集「被爆者が遺した最後の言葉」が放映されました。）

竹岡　誠治

ホスピタルの母

原稿を記す母

竹岡 智枝子

"戦争"とは。　メラ〜オスピタル5病棟

生きものすべてを不幸にするもの
先づは、生活用品そのものがすべて
軍用品になり、国民は食べ物一切が
配給となり草までも食べなければ…と
なり、遠くの農家まで行き頭を下げて大
きなふくろをかついで少しでも食べられるものを
もらって帰り近所の方達と分け合う。先づは子
供達に食べさせ残ったものを親達が食べるとい
うことです。着る物もなく、学用品もすべて学も
消してえんぴつ一本が、消しゴム一ケが宝物となり
ました。トイレットペーパーも新聞紙を使用してまし
た。今考えればよく生きてきたと思います。
原爆の時、私は十七才女学校五年でやっと身隊
して軍じん工場に行こうと家を出る所でした。
ピカッとドンをされきうきにも アッイよ、水よと云
つていけて…さけぶ人達に水を上げられなくて…
母はその時、すでに岡山陸軍病院看護婦としてのきんむ
火の中を毎日危島に…むいむ
日々で見つけましたが右服を負ぬき息赤い眼玉が
ポロンと光びておりました…
ましたが体内に危様に入り、カン車門区がかり三十年生きていき
ました。母は岡山陸軍病院に行きニ十年生きていた
だきました…私は21才で結婚し…ましたが今だ
日々食べては病死は原爆ようでした…
二度とふたび…戦争は絶対に許してはならない…

母の原稿1

平和運動へと!!

悲惨な苦しい終戦をむかえました
チャンスがやってきました。アメリカ
とって広島県代表として、S.G.I.のメンバー
被爆体験を話ることになり、その時のうれしる
格別のものでした。第三回特別軍縮
統会が二ケ年つづけられ各国々を
つなぐでいかに広島が苦しみを語り
広島県代表をして、私が被爆
体験を話ることになり、その時のうれしる
格別(ばくはつ)…は私が行かれ各国々が
…国々は素晴らしい国でして…
世界一の国で…天下地下鉄も地下
顔も教育も第一国を愛すことも…
ゴルバチョフさんでした。平和を愛す
人格者で偉く私達とお話をする
その後ゴルバチョフさんは日本にも来国され…
行為はとても大…ねも皆無で
国でしょうが、食べ物すらとてもおいしいです
車も三十年間で行き…の道とうでずらと…
以来三十年間にわたり広島平和への国に毎日行
和を祈りつづけ…私も元子…と…
皆様朝々なに世界平和をお祈りしましょう

母の原稿2

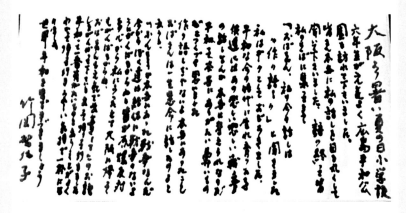

母の原稿3

はじめに

　新緑の季節も終わりに近づき、流れる風に少しばかりの湿った気配が混じるようになりました。東京で生活している六十歳になる息子から連絡があったのは、二週間ほど前、久しぶりに広島に行くので、そのときに私の体験を聞きたいという。思いがけない申し出でした。

　昨年、平成二十一年（二〇〇九年）五月のことです。

　五月の三十日と三十一日、土日にかけて友人とともに広島にくるという。三十日に私は若い人たちに、「国立広島原爆死没者追悼平和祈念館」でお話しをさせてもらうことになっています。ここに参加してもらうことにしました。

　市の西の端にある己斐上町から北部の高取に移り住んで、もう三十年になります。高取の家から車を運転してほぼ三十分。車窓を、少し花をつけはじめた夾竹桃が流れていきます。会場のある中島町の平和記念公園に着いたのは、午後二時十分ころでした。この日は二時半から、広島修道大学の学生さんたちに一時間ほど話を聞いてもらうことになってい

1

ます。

資料館東館の啓発担当の方にご挨拶して会場に向かうあいだ、どう伝えようか、なにを話そうか、今日はずっと気にかけていた息子に聞いてもらう。初めてのことです。どうしようかと、こころが揺れていましたが、いつもと同じにしようと決めました。ありのまま、正確に伝える、それがいい。

会場に着いてから、学生さんたちが入ってくるまで五分ほど、先にきて待っていた二人とすこしだけ会話を交わしました。どうしたのかと心配したのですが、体調も安定しているようです。

学生さんたちを引率している森島教授と、平和文化センターの木村主任に、息子たちが同席する許可をえました。すこし驚いていたようですが、こころよく応じてくださいました。席についた学生さんたちにも息子を紹介してくれます。私は、息子や娘の子どもたち、私の孫たちよりもっと若い方たちに語りはじめました。

「今日、みなさんにお話しするのは、暗い、哀しい内容です。私のちょうどみなさんと同じくらい、十七歳のときのことです。あの日の朝、私は──」

2

この日話を聞いてくれた息子の申し出を受け、私は手記を纏めることをこころに決めました。それから一年半、懐かしく、苦しく、せつなく、そして希望に輝く日々を過させていただきました。こうした機会を与えてくださったみなさまに感謝いたします。

平成二十二年（二〇一〇年）十月

竹岡智佐子

英語版出版にあたって

二〇一五年は、太平洋戦争終結七十周年となります。それはまた、広島・長崎への原子爆弾の投下から七十年でもあるのです。この本は、それによってもたらされた、十七歳の私が見た、この世の地獄の記録であり、その地獄から宿命を転換し、生きる希望と使命を見出した記録でもあります。

このたび、ぜひともこの記録を英文で出版するようにと、強い要請を各方面から受けました。

十七歳で被爆した私は、今年で八十七歳になりました。おかげさまで元気です。八十九歳になった夫の介護を続けながら、軽自動車を自分で運転し、被爆体験を、広島にお見えになる中学・高校の修学旅行生や、要望があると、全国の学校に出向き、生徒さんたちに直接、語り続けております。

さらに、広島市の制度で、被爆体験を語り継ぐ伝承者養成事業がスタートし、二〇一三年より、娘の東野真里子が、私の体験を公的に受け継いでくれることとなりました。また、

4

広島にいる孫の東野絵美も、一緒に私の体験を語り継ぐ決意を固めてくれました。これ以上の喜びはありません。

広島・長崎を史上最後の被爆地とするために、世界中の皆様に、なかでも、核保有国の方々にこの体験を読んでいただきたいものです。

五〇〇〇年前の古代エジプトの創世神話に、「太陽はロータスが生み出した」というものがあると、息子の誠治から聞きました。それは、「最初に現われた陸魂には蓮の花が咲いたという。その蓮のつぼみが甘味な香りを放ち、その花をひらきはじめると、太陽のレー（太陽神ラー）は蓮の花の中心から姿を現し世界に最初の光をもたらした」＊というものです。

この本が、小さいけれど、ロータスのつぼみになって、多くの次代を担う太陽を生み出す手助けとなることを、切に願っております。

この英語版の出版にあたって、ご尽力いただいた川村良子さん、そして、とりわけ格調高い翻訳をしていただいた、アンディ・クラークさんに、心から感謝申し上げます。

二〇一五年二月三日　広島にて

竹岡智佐子（たけおかちさこ）

＊クリスティーン・エルマディ「レーの創生神話」（アリス・ミルズ監修『世界神話大図鑑』荒木正純訳監修・東洋書林刊　所収）より

広 島 市 (1946)

0 1 2 3km
0.5 1.5 2.5

山陽本線

←宮島

広 島 湾

the US Army Map Service in 1946. より作成

(駅)	⑭観音橋	Ⓓ修道中学・高校
❶己斐駅	⑮相生橋	Ⓔ比治山学園
❷横川駅	(町・地区)	(病院)
❸広島駅	⑯己斐町	Ⓕ島外科病院
❹向洋駅	⑰己斐上町	Ⓖ舟入病院
(川)	⑱山手町	Ⓗ第1陸軍病院
⑤太田川	⑲鷹匠町	Ⓘ第2陸軍病院
⑥山手川／己斐川	⑳舟入町	Ⓙ日本赤十字病院
⑦福島川	㉑八丁堀	(その他)
⑧天満川	㉒新天地	Ⓚ中国電力
⑨本川	㉓白島町	Ⓛ中国新聞
⑩元安川	㉔段原町	Ⓜ福屋
⑪京橋川	(学校)	Ⓝ原爆ドーム
⑫猿猴川	Ⓐ己斐小学校	Ⓞ広島城
(橋)	Ⓑ江波小学校	Ⓟ縮景園
⑬己斐橋	Ⓒ山中高等女学校	

目次

ヒロシマの宿命を使命にかえて

原爆の語り部として生きる

竹岡智佐子

一

八月六日

私は、会場にきてくれた学生さんたちを見て、私の孫よりももっと若い方たちなのだと感慨を深くしながら話しはじめました。

　──私が今日みなさんにお伝えするのは、もう、暗い暗い戦争のお話しです。明るいことも楽しいこともない、嬉しいこともない、どうしても、暗くて悲しくて苦しいお話しばかりになります。私は夏場に入りますと毎年のように体調が崩れますが、みなさんも今日のように暑くなると同じでしょうから、気分が悪くならないように、どうか、楽な気持ちで聞いてください。

　みなさんもご存知のように、一九四五年、昭和二十年八月六日、午前八時十五分、この平和記念公園から東に少し出たところにある島外科病院、そのちょうど上空六〇〇メートルから八〇〇メートルの間で原子爆弾が炸裂しました。

　その一日前、五日の日に私は、大きな軍需工場になっていた東洋製罐の工場の中で兵器の部品を作っていました。

12

当時は中学校が四年間、もちろん男女共学ではないので、私は女学校を卒業しました。卒業するとすぐ、昭和十九年の四月から全員が陸軍か海軍の仕事をするようになっていました。女子挺身隊の一員になったのです。卒業したら、大学に行こうかな、私はなにになろうかな、といった自分のことは、いっさい考えられないのです。すべてが戦争、戦争を遂行することが最優先でした。戦争がはじまると、国民の生活に必要なものがどんどん失われていきます。お金から食糧から、衣類まで、すべて軍の関係に集められ使われてしまうので、なにもないのです。

いまの若い人たち、小学生さんたちは、きっと想像がつかないと思います。たった一本のエンピツが宝もので、消しゴムもたった一個、もう五ミリの玉になるくらいまで使わなければなりません。私が小学校の六年生になったころには、図画をするにも、絵の具もなく、画用紙も黒ずんだざらざらな紙で、すぐ破れてしまうようなものを使っていました。そういうように、なにもないなかで「戦争に勝たなくてはいけない」と、みんなが協力しながら、生きなければならない時代でした。

八月五日の日は朝早くから、自分で作ったハチマキを締めて、一所懸命、兵器の部品を

13

作ることに携わっていました。工員さんと同じように、大きなヤスリを使って、面取りという作業に懸命になります。夕方近くに「早く戦場に兵器を送らなければ、間に合わない。今夜は全員が徹夜作業だ」と告げられました。こうなっても、もちろん電話もないわけですから、今夜は家に帰れないと連絡もつけられないのです。でも、家の人たちは「忙しくて帰れないのだな」と分かってくれる。そういう時代でもありました。

私たちが作っていたのは、呉工廠で製造される人間魚雷「回天」の部品でした。せいぜい長さ十五メートル、幅もこの机くらい、直径一メートルのものに、たった一人が乗り込んで、敵の大きな軍艦に命中して沈める、自分の命もその場でなくなっていくという兵器です。一人で乗り込んでいく人のなかには、まだ中学校を卒業してわずか三か月の特訓を受けただけの人もいます。そうした、前途有望な多くの少年が、「お国のため」に多くの命を散らしていきました。

そうしたことを考えると、ああ戦争はいやだな、こんな兵器なんか作りたくないな、とみんな心の奥底では思っていました。でも、口に出してそんなことをいえば、たいへんなことになります。すぐに疑われて追及され、ついには警察や軍に連れていかれてしまう。ですから、みんな黙々と仕事をしました。

14

夜明け近くになって「女子挺身隊の人たちだけは、今日は家に帰ってゆっくり休んでください」となりました。八月六日の朝早くです。まだ夜も明けていないころです。

女子挺身隊の私たちは、帰らせていただける。もう、二か月も三か月もお休みがなかったので、さあ早く帰ろう、帰ろうと外に出て、いちばんに空を見ました。夏の夜明け前の空は、もうきれいで、一点の雲もなくきれいに星が輝いています。

「今日は暑くなりそうだわ。海水浴に行きたいよ」

でも、当時宮島の裏の海水浴場で泳いでいた人たちを、敵の飛行機が、グラマンという少し小型の飛行機ですが、低く飛んできて機銃掃射をし、水着のままの人たちが何人も撃ち殺されたことがありました。ですから、海水浴は禁じられていたのです。

「でも、海を見たいわね」

「行きましょう」

「行こう、行こう」

私をふくめて三人の仲好しで、宮島に行く約束をしました。

「八時十五分の電車に乗りましょう」

15

当時は、広島市のいちばん西の端になる己斐町から、宮島行きの電車が出るようになっていました。いまはJRで宮島行きがたくさんありますが。その己斐駅に八時十五分に集合しましょうとなりました。三人で、「そうしよう、そうしよう。うれしいね。よかったね」といいながら、工場を後にしました。

まだ夜は明けていないので、いったん己斐上町の家に帰り、洗濯をしたり、片づけをしていました。母は仕事が忙しく何日か家に戻れないでいます。一緒に暮らしていた祖母は七時半ごろに涼んでくるといって散歩に出かけました。家の片づけで忙しくしているとき、ふっと柱時計を見ると、もう八時十分になっています。

ああ、遅くなってしまった。十五分に電車に乗ろうといっていたのに、間に合わない、ああ、どうしよう。急いで玄関の外に立って、ポケットから小さな手鏡を出して顔を映しました。当時は髪も長くして三つ編みにしておりました。きれいに編めているのでよかったと思いました。

晴れあがった空を見上げてもう一度、ふっとなんの気なしに、手鏡を見たその時でした。

ピカッ！、ドーン。

うわっ！――頭をかかえたまま、なにも分からなくなってしまいました。

その後、何分が経過したのでしょうか。はっと気がついたとき、私はなぜそこに倒れているのか、まったく理解できませんでした。玄関前から、家の裏の方まで三〇メートルもあるサツマイモの畑の中に、私は倒れていました。

どうしたのか。ピカッ！、そうだ、私の家に焼夷弾が落ちたのだ、と思いました。当時、爆弾といえば焼夷弾でした。ほかの爆弾はなにも分かりませんので、そう思ったのです。すでに、東京も大阪も、岡山も焼夷弾で焼け野原になっていましたので、ついにその時がきたかと思ったのです。広島には呉の軍港がありますから、そのあたりも毎晩のように空襲警報が鳴り、焼夷弾が落とされていました。しかし、軍港があるのになぜか大規模な空襲はされていませんでした。

「焼夷弾だ。家に焼夷弾が！」

焼夷弾が落ちると、シュシュッという音がして、しばらくするとバッと炎が広がる、火が出たらすぐに水をかけて逃げる。そうした注意事項も何度か徹底されていましたので、

「あっ、いまならまだ火が出ていないから間に合う」

家の中には何箇所か防火用水としてバケツが置いてあります。

早く家の中に入って水をかけなければいけない。でも、足が立たない、どうしよう。ああ、頭もおかしいと思って、頭に手を当てました。すると、ズルーッと血が流れている。ああ、頭もやられたのだと思って、ふっと空を見上げました。

そこには、いままで見たことがない、真っ黒いような濃い灰色のような空です。雲なのか煙い渦を捲いて、どんどん広がっていきます。気持ちの悪い、怖ろしい原子なのか、その時は分からなかったのですが、それが放射能がいっぱい含まれていた原子雲だったのです。だれも知らなかったことです。ああ、怖ろしい、気持ち悪い、早く家の中に入りたい！

地面を這って、やっとの思いで傾いた家の中に入ってみると、二階に上る梯子段も斜めになり、何がどこにあるのか分からなくなっています。でも、一所懸命一階も二階も見て回ったのですが、どこにも、なんの音もしません。

「おかしい、これは焼夷弾ではないかもしれない」と外に出てみると、近所の方もみな出てきています。大きなガラスの三角形の破片が背中に食い込んで、血みどろになっているおばさん。大きな錆びついた釘が腐りかけたような板といっしょになって、横腹に突き刺さって血をどろどろ流しているおばさん。家の中にいた人はみなたいへんな怪我をして、

18

外に血みどろになって出てきています。

　ああ、おばさんたちがたいへんなことになる。釘やガラスを抜いて、止血をして薬を塗らなければ！　薬はなにもありません。消毒薬もありません。でも、水道がずっと出ていました。水道の水でどんどん流して洗ってから、止血をしよう。薬はなにもないのですから、普段から詳しい人に教わって止血の方法だけは、みなよく知っていたのです。

　「止血はきちんとしてくださいね。表通りに行って様子を見てくるからね」といって、私は少しはなれた道路まで行きました。すると、散歩にでかけていた祖母が帰ってきました。

　ああ、無事だった、よかった。祖母は己斐国民学校の脇を流れている川沿いを歩いていて、ちょうど橋の下にいたときに、爆弾が破裂したのでした。橋が陰になって爆風からも守られたのです。

　私が住んでいた己斐町は、爆心地から西三キロにありました。中心から二キロくらいまでの人は、ほとんどの方が即死、生きられた方も三時間か、長く生きられて六時間くらいで亡くなっています。

広島市は形状が円く、三方が山に囲まれた三角州にあります。たった一発の原子爆弾でも、太陽さえ出て、晴れてさえいれば爆撃はかならず成功する地形です。朝八時から三十分間は、山からの空気と海からの空気が、そろそろと入れ替わる時間で、風も吹かないのです。私は広島に生まれ育ってきましたが、朝の三十分間がそうした状態になるとは知りませんでした。ですから、アメリカ軍は、そこまでも微にいり細をうがって調べていたということです。

この二キロ以内には、陸軍の重要な司令塔になる施設が何箇所かあります。それも潰せるし住民も皆殺しにできる。まだ空襲をしていない日本の都市のなかで、アメリカ軍からみて、条件としてはいちばん広島がよかったのです。川は北側から、太田川が一本流れてきて、途中から七本に分かれている。現在は西側の二本が大きな一本になっていますので、六本ですが。海にも近い。

己斐町は、中心から三キロ、背後の山に抱えられ、夏場にはホタルも多く飛んでいる、静かな落ちついた町でした。家は己斐の駅から海側を背にして、なだらかな坂道を山に向かって十分ほど歩いたところにあります。

その坂道の道路に出て海の方に目をやりました。おかしい？　何か真っ黒い塊が、そろ

そろ、そろそろと上ってくる。あの黒い塊はなんだろう？　おかしいなと思ってみている

と、だんだん近づいてきます。

それは人間の集団でした。みんな真っ黒い大やけどを負っています。女の人は髪の毛を

逆立て、皮膚がずるずるに焼け爛れています。ちょうど海から若布を引き上げたような形

です。ぼろぼろに焼け爛れたその皮膚が、肩から腕を伝わって指の先から垂れ下がってい

るのです。そうした方たちの集団でした。

「熱いよう、助けて！」

「お母さん、苦しいよう！」

「お姉ちゃん、ノドが痛いよ！」

「お兄ちゃん、水が欲しいよ！」

「ノドが痛い、水！　水が欲しい！」

みんな、それぞれの家族の名前を呼んで、「熱い、熱い」「水！　水」と訴えています。

これは、たいへんなことだ。道路のすぐそばに大きな一軒の家があり、その家は屋根も

無事だったので、日を避けて陰に入るのでみなその家に入ろうとするのですが、そこまで

のあいだに、道路の真ん中のところで二十人も三十人も倒れていきました。

21

私はもうなにも考えられませんでした。夢中になってばたばたと駆け寄りました。ずるずるのやけどの人の肩をたたいて、「しっかりして！　死ぬんじゃないよ」と。「よくここまで逃げてきたね、一人ですか、どこから逃げてきたの。名前、名前は」

ついさっきまで、みんな家族の名前を呼んでいたのに、もう声が出ません。喉の中まで、ずっと焼け爛れてきたのです。

「みんな声が出ない、名前がいえない。でも、ここまで逃げてきたんだから、大丈夫よ、しっかりするのよ！」

近所のおばさんたちも、道路に出てきました。うわーっ、たいへんなことになった、ひどいことになった、早く助けてあげよう。どうしたら助けてあげられるか。まず、このやけどに薬を塗ってあげたい。でも、薬はどこにもない。私たちも水で洗っただけ。では、なにか食べさせてあげたい。食べれば元気がでて、生き延びれるかもしれない。でも、食べるものもほとんどなかったのです。食料の配給はもう一週間も遅れていました。私たちも今朝お水を飲んだきり、なにも食べていませんでした。

困った、どうするか。「じゃあ、お水、お水」と、やけどの人たちは「水が欲しい！」といったのだから、水道の水をどんどん運んできて、飲ましてあげたり、冷やしてあげたり、拭

22

いてあげたりしました。拭くといっても、みな重度のやけどですから、当たり前に拭いて
あげることはできません。タオルも、当時は「日本タオル」といって、ただの布切れなの
ですが、それも充分にはありません。その布をしめしては、胸の上に置いてあげたり、そっ
と頭の上に置いてあげたりするしかできませんでした。

そして、少し時間が経ったころ、さあーっと、あたりが陽が暮れるように暗くなってき
ました。どうしたのか？　「まだ、朝よね」「そうよ、朝よ」。腕時計もなにもありませんから、
確実な時間は分かりません。「まだ朝よ」「そうよ、朝よ」と言い合うばかりですが、あた
りはどんどん暗くなっていきます。と思ったら、真っ黒い雨が、ざーざーと激しく降って
きました。「黒い雨」でした。

爆弾が炸裂したときに、人間も家も、ほこりもなにもかも吸い上げ、それが真っ黒い雲
となって、北西に流れてきたのです。私たちが住んでいた己斐町が、ちょうどその雲の通
り道にあたったのです。私が畑に倒れていたときに見た、あの気持ちの悪い、恐ろしい渦
が雲となり、真っ黒い雨となって降ってきたのです。

「いやあ、気持ち悪いね。みんな、こっちにきて、家の庇の中に」といっても、道路の中
央で倒れて動けないのですから、みんなその黒い雨にうたれてしまいました。私たちの腕

23

や足にくっついた雨は、大豆のように円く、拭いても水で流しても取れません。

そして、だんだんと時間が経って、あたりに本当の夕闇が迫ってきました。そのとき一人の人が、すうーっと私の前に立って、「ちいちゃーん」というのです。えっと思いました。私の名前を呼んだのです。全身真っ黒こげで、だれなのかまったく分かりません。頭も真っ黒こげで、近寄ってみますと、髪の中にはカリカリのようなものがくっついている、そこにあの黒い雨が降ったので、もうどろどろになって、頬は裂けて血が流れている。よく見ると、胸から背中にかけて小さな穴が無数に開いている。その穴から全部、血が吹き出ている。

「いやあ、ひどくやられたね。あっ、あなたホコ（美保子）ちゃんじゃない。命があってよかった。よくここまで逃げてきたね」

薬も食べるものもありませんが、私の家に連れて行って、中に入れて水で冷やしてあげるだけでした。その子は、宮島に行く約束をして己斐の駅で待ち合わせた二人のうちの一人でした。広島市内の天満町の先に住んでいたのですが、朝、市街電車に乗って己斐に向かう途中、被爆して電車の窓から外に吹き飛ばされたのです。そこまでは分かっていたのですが、あとはまったく分からないといいます。はっと気づいたときは、川に落ちていた。

電車の止まったところから、川までは一キロメートルもあるのですが、風速二〇〇メートルから三〇〇メートルという、もの凄い爆風ですから一瞬で飛ばされていたのです。

「でも、命があってよかった、よかった」

私たちがいた部屋の隣りに小さな部屋があり、ふっとそちらに、なにか黒いものがうごめく気配がしました。おかしいな、家には祖母と私しかいなかったのに、だれかいるのかなと思って見ると、十三人、ずるずるの大やけどで真っ黒の人たちがいました。喉は張り裂けそうでチリチリ痛み、全身の痛みをどうしたら少しでも楽になるかと思って、隣同士で腕をすり合わせるようにしていました。

「みなさん、よくここまで逃げてきましたね。いまお水を飲ましてあげますからね。大丈夫よ」と、一人ずつお水を飲ませましたが、半数の人はもう息がありませんでした。生きている方たちに、なにか食べさせてあげたいが、なにもありません。

「名前は？」――そうだ、声が出なくても、メモ用紙とエンピツがあれば、名前は書けると思い、持っていきました。エンピツを握らせようと思って指を見ますと、五本の指の骨が融けかかってずるずるになって、エンピツも持つことができません。そして、だんだん眼も動かなくなってきます。耳ももう聞えなくなっていたのかもしれません。どんなにし

25

ても「名前だけは」と思ったけれど、それも許されませんでした。ああ、残念！　せっかくここまで逃げてきたのだから、名前だけは教えてほしかった。

これだけたくさんの人が、どんどんと山側に上ってきたということは、広島市内はいったいどうなっているのか？「みんな、死なないでね。私は山に登って見てきますから」といって、家の裏側の山に向かいました。そのころは、みな外で遊ぶ時代ですので、子どもたちが、上の中腹から尻にゴザを敷いて滑り降りる遊びをしていたところです。その山の頂上に登ってみました。

すると、広島市内が全部、夕暮前の薄明かりのなかですが、手に取るように見えました。ほとんど何も残っていません。ゾオッとしました。中国新聞社は鉄筋コンクリートでしたから三分の一ほど残っていて、福屋デパートが少し残っていたのですが、あとは、ほとんど焼け爛れた荒地。今朝方まで何万人もの人が生活し働いていたあの広島市内に一軒も残っていないのです。全滅です。

うわーっ、これは焼夷弾ではない。なにか大きな爆弾を落とされたに違いない。そう思ってずうーっと一望すると、相生橋が見えます。現在の平和記念公園の少し北側にある、広島市でいちばん大きな橋です。相生橋が見えて、川が見えます。水は見えないのですが、広

あれが川だと分かるのです。そこから東の方に目を移すと、広島城や護国神社があるあたりに、広い敷地をもつ陸軍病院があったのですが、影も形もありません。

「ああ、どうしよう、丸焼けになっている。お母さん！　生きていてね！」

私の母は、陸軍病院の看護婦、婦長をしていたのです。もう一週間も家には戻れないで、そのころはもう、外地から負傷した兵隊さんが毎日帰ってきます。ああ、お母さんも！

病院のあたりにはなにもありません。ああ、お母さんも！

「明日の朝になったら助けに行くから、死ぬんじゃないよー」

七日の朝早く、夜が明けるのを待って、家のことを祖母に頼んで一人で広島市内に向かいました。水をびしゃびしゃになるほどかけた防空頭巾をかぶって、もうぼろぼろになっている靴を履いていきます。靴は当時は一足買ったら何年も履くようなときです。お金もないですし、なにより品物がないのですから。破れたところに継ぎをあてがって、そこが破れたらまた布をあてがって、裏には二箇所も三箇所も穴が開いているので、雨のときは中がぐしゃぐしゃになるような靴です。でも、火の中に行くのだから裸足よりも履いていたほうがいいと思い、それを履いて、水筒を肩からかけて家を出ました。

家のある山側の己斐上町から、まず下の己斐の町に降りていきました。己斐は爆心地から三キロ離れており、市の西側の大きな川を越えた場所ですので、火の粉も飛んできてはいませんでした。焼けてはいません。でも、あの爆風で多くの家が潰れ、残った家も斜めになったりしていました。潰れた家の下敷きとなった女の方の「助けて！ここにいるのよ」という声がきこえます。でも、その声もだんだん小さくなっていきます。火のないところで、目の前に助けを求める人がいるのに、助けてあげることができませんでした。

当時、国内に残っていたのは、幼い子ども、国民学校の生徒、おじいちゃん、おばあちゃん、そして力の弱い女性たちだけです。食べ物もあまり口にしていないので、みなふらふらとしながら柱を動かそうとするのですが、大きな柱を五本も六本も持ち上げなければなりません。だんだん小さくなる声を聞きながら、助けてあげることができなかったのです。こうして亡くなっていった気のどくな女の方が、何人もいました。

その場所を過ぎ己斐橋を渡り、次の川に出ました。橋が半分流れてしまい渡れません。どこで泳いでもいいですよ。川で泳いでもいいですよという時期がありましたので、そういうときは私たちは満潮の時を狙って、欄干の上から飛び込んで遊んだ川です。その懐かしい木の橋が、半分流れてしまっています。よし！ 泳ごうと小さな木の橋があります。

決めて川の半分くらいまでいくと、何人かの女の人が浮いたり沈んだりしながら流れてきます。「あっ、お母さんかもしれない」と思い、急いで泳いでいくと四人とも髪の長い人でした。母ではありません。母は髪を短く揃えて仕事をしていました。

そこを離れて、向こう岸から半分残った橋によじ登りました。私は十七歳の娘でしたが、よく分かっている橋でしたのでよじ登ることができました。やっとその川を渡り、市の中心に向かいました。次の橋、次の橋、三つの橋を渡ったところに女子挺身隊で働いていた工場があります。爆風で全倒壊しぺしゃんこになって、あちこちで機械の油が臭く燃えつづけています。「昨日の夜明け前、女子挺身隊の私たちは工場を出たが、残った工員さんたちはどうなったか」「あのまま朝まで作業を続けていたら、私も死んでしまっていただろう」。でも、まだ助けをもとめている人がいるかもしれないと思い、広い工場の敷地をぐるぐると廻りました。どこにも、だれも人間はいません。私がたった一人、防空頭巾をかぶって歩いていました。

どこにも人間がいなくなっています。どちらかいい方向に逃げたのかもしれない。どの方向に逃げたのだろう、と思いながら、どんどんと中心地に向かい、相生橋まできました。ふっと川を見ました。川といっても海が近いですから満ち干きがあります。ちょうど

29

満潮時でした。でも、川の「水」が見えません。見渡すかぎり上流から下流まで、びっしりと「人間」が並んで材木や筏のようになって、死んで浮かんでいたのです。絶対になにか大きな爆弾に違いない。ぶるぶると震えだす身体を押さえながら、人が浮かんでいる川に向かって「お母さん！お母さん！」と何度か大声で呼んでみましたが、返事があるわけもありません。どうやって母を捜したらいいのだろう。どこかにボートはないか。いや、ボートがあってもだめだ。これだけ多くの人が浮かんでいるのだから、ボートが進む余地もない。だれか歩いている人がいたら、だれでもいいから、いっしょに母を捜してもらおう。しかし、どこを見ても、見回しても、人間はやはり私だけ、たった一人しかいません。

近くに浮かんでいる人をよく見ると、全身のやけどです。身体はちりちり、じりじりと痛い、水が欲しい。もう川に飛び込むほかになかった。次から次に飛び込んで川の水をガブガブ飲んで、息絶えたのでしょう。みなブクブクに膨れ上がっています。頭も顔もドッチボールのようになって、だれがだれやらまったく見分けもつきません。

ああ、困った。どうして母を捜していいのか分からない。生きて歩いているのは私一人だけ。川土手を上流に向かって歩き、川向こうを見ると、円い屋根の産業奨励館だけが、

30

建物の屍のように残っていました。さらに遠くに目を移すと男の人が三人、真っ裸になって、川から死体を引き上げているのが見えました。あっ、あのあたりは陸軍病院だ。早く行って聞いてみれば、なにか、母のことが分かるかもしれないと急ぎました。

相生橋を半分渡ったところに、三人、真っ黒こげの人が倒れていました。駆け寄って体をたたいて「しっかりするんですよ！」と声をかけましたが、うっすらと開いている眼はまったく動きません。何時間か前に息絶えたのでしょうか。どうしてあげることもできません。相生橋の欄干は石造りでしたが、全部落ちてしまい一本も残っていませんでした。やっと橋を渡りきって、あの三人のところに行きました。

三人はびっくりして、「おっ、お姉ちゃん、どこからきた！　どこもやけどもしていないね」「服も着ているね！」。不思議だ、不思議だといいます。

「はい、私は己斐の山の上から、母を捜してここまできました」

「そうか！　お母さんは、陸軍病院の看護婦さんなのか。それではお母さんはもう生きてはいないかもしれない。今朝早くまでは、何百人かの人がまだ生きていたが、みんな次から次に、口からも、鼻からも、耳からも血を吹いて死んでいった」といいます。

生きている四、五十人の人は集まっているが、もうだれがだれやら分からない姿になっ

て、息も弱く、死を待つばかりになっている。「お姉ちゃんのお母さんが、生きていると は考えられない」。川に浮かんでいるか、病院の下敷きになって死んでいるかどっちだ から「お姉ちゃん、早く己斐に帰りなさい」というのです。

「お姉ちゃん一人だけでも、助からなければいけないよ。もし敵機がくれば、空からは丸 見えだ、すぐに撃たれてしまう。早く帰りなさい！」

はい、といって帰りかけたとき、「お姉ちゃん、おいで、ちょっと」というので戻ると、「せっ かく遠くからきたのだから、いまここに並べた死体を見ていきなさい。お母さんがいるか もしれないから」といいます。でも、どの人も凄い姿で、見分けもつきません。

「お母さんは、なにか分かる目印があったかい」

「目印といっても、とくにはないですよ」

「よく考えてごらん。なにかあるだろう」

「あっ、そういえば母は金歯を三本入れていました！」

そうだ、歯を調べようと、木切れを拾って、死体の五人、十人、三十人、四十人と口を 開けて調べていきました。なかなか口も開きません。唇も膨れ上がっていて三センチくら いしか中は見えません。それは、それはとても人間の姿とは思えないようになってしまっ

32

ています。

「お姉ちゃん、見つかった？　金歯の人いた？」

「うん、いません」

「そうだろう。早く帰りなさい」といわれました。

三人は、病院の衛生兵という兵隊さん。ケガもやけども軽かったので、なにかしなければ死んでいった方々に申し訳ないと思い、川に浮かんだ人を引き上げていたのです。もし家族の人が捜しにきて、一人でも二人でも分かって会えれば、それは嬉しいことだと、その作業をつづけていたのです。

私はそこから離れ、きた方向に戻り、相生橋を渡りました。爆心地から五〇〇メートルも離れていない場所です。当時、国民学校の四年生の女の子と叔母がいました。

このあたりだと周囲を見渡していると、水槽に墨で書いた名前を見つけました。やはり、ここだ！　朝八時過ぎなら、食べるものはなくても茶の間あたりで水でも飲んでいたかもしれない。茶の間の跡あたりに埋まっているかもしれないと思い、おおよその見当をつけて掘ってみました。ぼろぼろの靴の先で掘りました。瓦礫も石もまだ熱をもっていました

ので、足の先をやけどしてしまいました。

懸命に掘りつづけ、やっと見覚えのある石の門柱を見つけ、茶の間あたりの瓦礫や石など被さったものを除けてみると、その下から小さな布切れが出てきました。叔母の服の布です。周囲をさらに掘ってみますと、二人は向かい合って座ったまま亡くなっていました。

すでに骨になっています。腰の骨の上に頭蓋骨がそのまま乗っています。

熱線が凄いものだったのです。太陽の熱が八千℃、原子爆弾が上空六〇〇メートルで爆発したときが六千℃、その熱が地上に降りてきたときは四千℃といわれます。そんな想像もできない熱で焼かれて、生きていられるわけもありません。逃げる暇もなにも、どうすることもできなかったのです。私は二人を見つけてあげてよかったと思います。二人の骨を拾ってあげられる。川に浮かんだ人たちは姿も変わり果て、だれやらさえ分からなくなっています。

私は、静かに手を合わせて、二人の骨のいくつかをハンカチで丁寧に包みました。叔母の家から帰ろうとしたとき、空襲警報のサイレンが鳴りました。先ほどから東の方からきているのは気づいていましたが、もう上空にきています。どこかに隠れなければいけない。ずうっと遠くを見ると、大きな水槽が半分周囲には隠れるところはどこにもありません。

壊れているのがあります。あっ、あそこに行ってかがもうと。かがんでも空からは丸見えなのでしょうが、もし爆弾を落とされたら、回りになにもないよりは命を守れるととっさに思って、やけどした足で駆け込んで、身を隠すようにしました。

そこで、ふと下を見ると人がいます。若いお母さんが赤ちゃんを抱いて死んでいました。

ああ、可哀相に、若いお母さんは必死になって赤ちゃんを守り、守ってここまで逃げてきて、ここにたどり着いて息絶えて亡くなったのだ。赤ちゃんの足が二本、お母さんの焼け爛れた胸の下から覗いていましたが、きれいな足でやけどはしていません。片方の足にはガラスの破片が食い込んでケガしていましたので、どこか家の中で涼しい場所に寝かされていたのを、お母さんが引っぱって助け出し、ここまで抱いてきたのかもしれない。

赤ちゃんは生きているかもしれないと思い、引っぱり出して胸に抱きました。でも、すでに息もなく、冷たい体になっていました。冷たくなった赤ちゃんを抱きしめていたその時、私ははっと、われに返りました。「われに返る」というのを初めて実感しました。昨日から、やけどの人たちを助けなければ、お母さんを捜しに行かなければ、川には人が死んで一面を覆って浮かんでいる、もうただ一所懸命で、なにも考えられなくなっていたのです。

冷たくなった赤ちゃんを抱きしめていた時、初めて怒りが込み上げてきました。泣けて泣けて仕方がありません。涙がぼろぼろと出てきます。なんと可哀相な、なんの罪もないこの赤ちゃんまで、なぜ殺さなくてはならないのか!「ああ、こんな戦争をだれがしたんだ! 私は絶対に許さない! アメリカだろうが、日本だろうが絶対に許さない!」という気持ちが、胸いっぱいに広がったのです。

その母子となかなか離れられなかったのですが、やっと気持ちの整理がついて、二人に別れを告げて、己斐の家に戻りました。家には親戚の五人のおばさんたちが山伝いにたどり着いていました。二人はもう息をするのもやっとで、水を飲ます間もなく亡くなってしまいました。三人はなんとか命をとり止めました。

私は、あくる日、八日にも母を捜しに出かけました。昨日は相生橋を渡って左側を捜したのだから、今日は右に行こう。右に行くと広島市でもいちばんの繁華街の地域です。そういう人たちの面倒を見る人もいないで、みな死んでしまっている。私は一人ひとり、母ではないかと見ていきました。二十人も三十人も、真っ黒になって道にころがっています。この人も違う、この人もやはり違う、あっこの人は頭の格好が母に似ているが、やは

り違う。ふっと気がつくと、川底で生き残ったドブネズミ三匹が、亡くなった人たちを食べていた。ああっ、情けない。戦争したらこんな目に遭うのだ。

なんともいえない気持ちで、南の方にずうっと歩いていくと、気がついたら日赤病院の焼け跡に出ていました。そこには、大きな人間の山ができていました。亡くなった人を積み重ねて焼くのです。二つの山にはもう火がついています。もう一つの山にいまから火をつけるときでした。「ちょっと待ってください。お母さんを捜しにきたのです」とお願いして、死体の山の回りをぐるぐる巡って、母ではないか、この人は母ではないかと目を凝らしました。いくら廻って見ても、どの人も顔の形も崩れて、まったく分かりません。

「ああ、お母さん、ごめんね。今日も見つけてあげることができなかった」と苦しい胸を抱えながら、家に帰りました。

家に戻ると連絡が入りました。近くにきれいな緑に包まれた己斐の国民学校があります。その校庭に大きな穴をたくさん掘ったので、亡くなった方を運んでくださいという。まだ斜めになった家の中に、いま死んだ、昨日亡くなったという多くの人がおりました。名前も分からない気の毒な方たちが、どんどん学校の校庭に運ばれてきます。あのきれいな校庭が、なんとその夜には、二千人ともいわれる人たちの焼き場になったのです。

じつに凄惨な光景でした。こんなことになろうとは、私は思ってもみませんでした。あ

あ、こんな戦争、早く終ってしまえ！　と再び強い怒りが込み上げてきます。

　翌日の九日は南側、観音橋の方に母を捜しに出かけました。真ん中が折れかかって曲がっ

た橋の上から川を見ると、布団にくるまった死体が浮かんでいます。長い髪の毛が水に揺

れていました。母ではないことはひと目で分かりました。母は見つかりません。私は昼ご

ろから吐き気がつづき気持ちが悪くなっていました。おばさんたちのやけどや傷はひどいこ

とが気にかかり、そのまま家に帰りました。家に避難しているおばさんたちのこ

ています。傷口からうみが出て悪臭が家中に漂っています。傷の中にはうじ虫がわいてい

ました。

　十日の日も少し捜しに出ましたが、体がいうことをききません。もうふらふらになって、

歩くと胸がむかむかします。夜になって、頭に手を当てるとずきずきと痛みます。痛み止

めもなく、どうしようとまた手を頭にやると、バサッと手のひらいっぱいに髪の毛が抜け

てきます。ああっ、気持ち悪い、どうしたのかと腕を見ると、小さな卵くらいの形で、薄

い紫色の斑点が三つも四つも両腕に出ています。私も病気になって、死んでしまうかもし

れない。「お母さん！　ごめんなさい。明日は捜しに行けないかもしれない」。でも、生き

38

ていてね。生きていれば、かならず私が捜しますから、と心のなかで叫びました。

そのとき、近くに高林さんという大きな農家の家があって、そこのおじいさんがやってきました。

「ちいちゃん、毎日お母さんを捜して、見つからないのか。明日も捜しに行くの？」

「うん、明日はもう行けないかもしれない。身体も具合が悪くなって変な斑点が出て、髪の毛も抜けて。気分も悪いし、出かけられそうもないんです」

「そうか。でも、お母さんはどこかに生きておられて、捜しにくるのを待っているかもわからんぞ。元気出して捜しに行きなさい。明日はこのじいさんもついていってやるから、朝から行こう」──こう励ましてくれました。

次の日、八月十一日は夜が明けるのを待って、今度は市の西の方に出かけました。それまでに広島駅を中心とする市の中央方面は全部まわっていたのです。西の方面に向かう途中、一人のおじさんに会いました。

「あんたたちは、だれかを捜しているのか。それならこの川を伝って、海の方向に行きなさい。江波の国民学校に収容されている人たちがいる」といいます。江波の学校には、た

39

くさんの死人と、死にそうになっている人がいるという。

二人で急いで行ってみると、学校の中はもう廊下も歩けないほど、死んだ人でいっぱいになっています。あちらこちらに、五人も六人も重なって亡くなっていて、さまざまな方向を向いています。見分けもつかなくなっているのを、下を向いている人を上に向かせたりしながら、一人ひとり確認していきました。まったく分かりません。すでに六日目になっていますので、生きている人でさえ、負傷した箇所から体が腐りはじめている状態なのです。

もう学校の中には、息もできないほどの悪臭が漂っています。死体にも生きている人にも、真っ黒にハエがたかっています。

おじいさんは、全教室を母の名を呼んで回っていました。いままでどの教室でもだれも手を上げる人も声をあげる人もいないという。最後の教室でした。ここで分からなかったら、今日はもう帰ろうと話し合っていました。教室の中には何箇所か、いくつかの机を寄せて、その上に生きているのか亡くなっているのか分からない人たちが乗せられていました。

私は教室のいちばん前の机の上にいる人たちの傍に立っていました。おじいさんが母の名前を教室中に分かるように叫びました。

「おーい、おリョウさんや。ちいちゃんが捜しにきたぞ。おリョウさんはおらんか、おっ
たら返事をしてくれ！」

おじいさんの声が聞こえたのでしょうか、私の近くの人が、かすかに頭を動かしました。

そして、虫のなくようなか細い声を出しました。

「ちいちゃん」

母でした！　二人で、曲げている足をゆっくり伸ばしてみると、真っ黒にたかっている
ハエの間から看護婦の制服が分かりました。母でした！　頭から顔中包帯で巻かれていま
した。だれかが捲いてくれていたのです。口の辺りの包帯を少しゆるめて口の中を覗いて
みると、金歯が三本見えました。母でした！

全身、黒こげのようになって、固まった血でカチカチになっています。母に間違いない。

さらに確認するために少し見えている看護婦の制服を引っぱりました。そのとき、ぼたぼ
たと、何百匹ものうじ虫がこぼれ落ちてきました。背筋が凍りつくような、悲惨な光景で
した。でも、母は生きていました！

おじいさんは、ポケットからトマトを二つ出しました。農家をしていたおじいさんは、
母がみつかったら食べさせようと、持ってきていたのです。もう六日もなにも食べていな

41

母は、ゆっくりとトマトを食べました。「もうこれで、死ぬわけにはいかんぞ。明日の朝大八車で迎えにくるから、死んではいかんぞ」と母に言い残して、おじいさんは己斐に戻っていきました。

その晩、江波の学校に残った私は、「お母さん、お母さん」と声をかけながら、母にたかっているハエを一匹ずつ、一匹ずつ取りつづけました。大きなハエで母の肉に喰らいついていて、なかなか取れません。指先に力を込めて引っぱると、母の焼け爛れた皮膚を口いっぱいにくわえて取れます。ハエを全部取りのぞくのに二時間以上かかりました。取り終えて母の身体を見て、びっくりしました。右半身が真っ黒に、ずるずるの大やけどを負っています。火の中を自力でくぐり、くぐり抜けて、やっと建物の外に出たのです。体の左側にはガラスの破片がいっぱい刺さっていました。

あくる朝早くおじいさんが迎えにきました。いっしょに大八車に母を乗せてやっと家に帰り着きました。近所のおばさんたちも、みんな道路に出て迎えてくれました。「よかった、生きていてよかった」。斜めに傾いた家に入って、母の治療をはじめました。母の包帯を取っていたおばさんが、ぎゃーと叫んで動けなくなってしまいました。なにがあっ

たのかと訝しく思いましたが、包帯を取り除いて驚きました。右の眼球がはじけて飛び出している、顔中にガラスが突き刺さっていて、鼻は折れて上からと下からとの二箇所、骨が覗いていました。母は息をするのもやっとのことだったのです。

母を連れ帰ったその日、八月十二日に己斐国民学校に母を診てもらいに行ったところ、何百人ものけが人がおり、私たちは四時間待ってやっと順番がきました。母の顔の包帯は巻き直して、息ができるように口元だけ出すようにしていました。医者も疲れはてており、包帯を解いた母を診て、飛び出している右の眼球に声を出していました。外科ではなく内科のお医者さんのようで、処置もすることなく少しだけ薬を塗って、看護婦さんがすぐに包帯を巻いて、ほんの数分で診察が終わりました。後ろには順番を待っているたくさんの方が控えています。

学校を出て家に戻るあいだに、母が「いまのは、土居の先生の声だった」というのです。私はもう長いこと父には会っていなかったので「まさか」と思いました。母を家に連れ帰って、すぐに小学校に行ったのですが、すでにほかのお医者さんと交替しております。

「前の先生はどこに宿泊していたのですか」と聞くと、大きな地主の岩原のお宅だという。岩原の家には、私と同じ山中高等女学校で一級上の娘、ひでちゃんがいます。家にうかが

43

うと、ちょうどひでちゃんがおりました。

「土居盛登先生がお宅に宿泊していたの？」と聞くと、「そうよ、ついさっきトラックが着いて、新しい先生がきて、そのトラックに土居先生が乗って行ったところよ」という。

「土居先生は、私の父なのよ」

「ええっ、それなら引き止めておいたのに！ 知らなかったから」

母は変わり果てた姿になっていましたし、ひどい混乱のなかで、分からなかったのです。

土居の父は、岡山の上伊福で医者をしていたのですが、無二の親友の方のすすめで、広島県の忠海——呉線で竹原と三原の中間になる忠海に移転していました。壊滅した広島市内に郡部の医者が派遣になり、父は一人の看護婦とともに、十二日には己斐国民学校でけが人の手当てをしていたのです。二か月のちに、一人で忠海の父に会いに行ったとき、このことを告げると、父も本当に驚いていました。

六日間、捜して、捜して、やっと見つけて連れ帰った母に、満足に食べさせるものはありません。お米の一粒もないのです。水が出ていたことは本当に有り難かったのですが、そういう状態でした。このままでは、食べさせることもできない、治療することもできない。困り果てていたとき、通りかかった一人のおじさんが教えてくれました。広島市を通

り抜けてさらに行くと、戸坂という村がある。「その戸坂の学校に、早くお母さんを連れて行きなさい」といわれました。戸坂の学校には陸軍病院の医薬部が疎開しているという。

そこなら、医者も看護婦もおり、薬も食べ物もあるというのです。

今度は母をリヤカーに乗せて、私が自転車をこいで行きました。焼け跡をいくのでなかなか進みません。三時間かかって、ようやく戸坂の学校に着きました。すると、中から兵隊さんが出てきて「困ったなー。けが人を連れてきたのか」といいます。軍医も看護婦もいたが、つい少し前にみんな、口から血を吐いて死んでしまったのだという。獣医さんが一人だけ生き残っていました。母の眼を診てくれたのは、その獣医さんでした。すぐに母の右目の摘出手術をするといいます。

教室の床の上にむしろを敷いて、生き残った四人の衛生兵が母の体を押さえつけ、獣医さんが母の顔の右脇に立ちました。そのとき、母は左目を見開いて獣医さんを見て叫びました。

「やめてください！　私はこの手術は絶対に受けませんから！」

母は看護婦、婦長をしていましたから、その獣医さんをひと目見て、どんな手術をされるのかが分かったのだと思います。私ももう十七歳になっていましたから、分かりました。

45

麻酔薬もなにもありません。獣医さんの右手を見ると、たった一本の小さなメスが握られています。このメス一本で、母の右目は生身のままくり抜かれるのです。ああっ、どうしよう！

そのとき、獣医さんがゆっくり説明してくれました。強い光線が右目に入って眼球がはじけて飛んで出ている。しかし、中ではつながっている。こういう場合は早く摘出しなければ左の目も見えなくなってしまう、と説明してくれました。

「お母さん、広島市は全滅して、お医者さんはもう一人もいないのよ。いまここで手術をしてもらわなければ、左の目も見えなくなるのよ。勇気をだして、絶対に大丈夫だから！」

私は一所懸命に励まして、母を説得しました。手術の間は、私は教室の廊下に出て終るのを待ちました。母のうめき声、あばれる音、叫び声を聞きながら、私は目を伏せじっと堪えていました。心のなかで「どうか、母を助けてください、母を」と祈りつづけていました。どれほどの時間が経ったのでしょうか、周りはとっぷりと日が暮れています。衛生兵の方がきて、手術の終ったことを告げられました。

「終了したよ。今晩はここで休んで、明日の朝、連れて帰りなさい」

母を家に連れ帰ってからが、また大変でした。斜めになった家に入りたがりません。家

46

に入るとまた爆撃にやられる、とこわがります。母は大やけどを負っているうえに、生身のまま右目をくり抜かれています。その全身の痛みを訴えます。体を横たえても痛みます、じっとしていても痛みます。私のほうも、身体に薄紫色の斑点が出ています、髪の毛は抜けつづけ、吐き気もとまりません。

そのとき、私は思いました。これこそが生き地獄なのだ。母と私はいま、生き地獄にいる。こんな生き地獄を、どこの国の人にも、二度と遭わすことはできない。絶対にこんな戦争をさせてはいけない。

このときはもう、原子爆弾と分かっていました。こんな恐ろしい爆弾、一度に二十万もの人を殺してしまう爆弾、絶対に許してなるものか。この戦争、負けるなら早く負けてしまえ！　早く負ければ、一人でも多くの人が助かる、と思いました。そして、かならず原爆を落としたアメリカに行って、この惨状を伝えようと決めました。食料もない、なにもない。生き残った国民は、食べ物を漁って歩いている。本当にみじめな姿になってしまっていました。

二　戦後

私の母、國貞リョウは明治三十六年（一九〇三年）四月の生まれ、昭和二十年の当時は四十二歳、広島第一陸軍病院の婦長をしておりました。一人娘の私は、母より十八歳年長の父・土居盛登とのあいだに、昭和三年二月三日に生まれております。土居の父は岡山の病院の内科医でした。

八月六日のあの日、母は爆心地から北一キロ以内にあった陸軍病院で勤務に就いているはずでした。私が何日も母を捜して歩いたのは己斐橋を渡ってから、東そして北の区域でした。その母がなぜ、陸軍病院からはるか南の天満川と本川にはさまれた河口付近の江波の学校に収容されていたのか。

母は江波に近い舟入病院に派遣されていたのです。それまで陸軍病院に入院していた、病いの重くなった連隊長の夫人が伝染病に罹っていることが五日に判明し、舟入病院に移されることになりました。舟入病院には隔離病棟があったのです。婦長なら任せられるということで、母は六日の早朝に夫人とともに舟入病院に移動していました。六日の朝、夫

人を病室に寝かせてから、母は夫人に読んで聞かせようと新聞を取りに事務所に行っていました。空襲警報も遠ざかり、今日はいい天気だなと右側の窓を半分開けて空を見上げたその時、爆発の強烈な光線が右目を刺し貫いたのです。母の左顔面に突き刺さっていた破片は事務所の窓ガラスでした。

重度の原爆症となった母の治療は、何年もつづくのですが、右目をくり抜いたあと、右半身の大やけど、そして体の左側に食い込んでいるガラスの除去からはじまりました。破片は皮膚の表面だけでなく、奥深くにも入り込んでいました。取り除いたのは顔面だけでも二十を超えました。全身にはいったいどれほどのガラスが食い込んでいたのか。

当初、気も狂わんばかりの痛みにさいなまれていた母は、よく耐えたと思います。壊滅した広島の地での治療です。薬などあるわけもなく、母は自分のそれまでの看護婦としての知識の全部を使って私に教え、治療をはじめました。手当ての方法、包帯の巻き方、湿布のやり方、痛みをどう除いていけばいいのか、すべて当時、母から教わったことです。

女学校時代の私は、父や母のように医療に携わり、医者になりたいと思い勉強に励んでいました。母の指導の下で、母の看護をつづけているとき、戦争によってとうとう医学の道に進むことはできなかったのですが、思いは果たされたと感じていました。生まれてか

らすぐ、何箇所かの親戚の家にあずけられ育ってきた私ですが、このときに思いは果たさ
れたのです。

　私が生まれたのは、広島市内のいちばんの繁華街になる八丁堀でした。母は当時は看
護婦会に所属して、そのつど派遣されながら看護婦の仕事をしておりました。八丁堀でガ
ラス店を営んでいた母の弟、叔父が私の面倒をみてくれました。そのあとに母の兄、伯父
夫婦が住む段原で育てられました。伯父は広島駅の助役をしておりましたので、段原の地
は交通の便もよかったのです。

　伯父夫婦には子どもがおりませんでした。私は生まれつき体が弱く、冬になると肺炎を
起こしていました。やはり、母親から離されて親戚に預けられているという、不安もあっ
たのでしょう。肺炎を起こし、辛子を溶いたものを胸に張って、沸かした湯気で部屋をみた
して治療してくれます。あまりに肺炎を頻発するものですから、この娘は育っていっても
肺病になるだろう、もういまのうちに余所にやったほうがいいと、伯母がいいだしたよう
です。肺病は当時は不治の病のように、やっかい扱いされていましたから。

　親戚がみな集まって、話し合いをします。父の知り合いに岡山の大きな病院をやってい

52

る人がいる。そこには子どもがいないので、連れて行ったらどうかとなりました。伯母と母に連れられて岡山まで行きました。私は眼も大きく、病弱であまり外にも出てませんから色白で、可愛らしく見えたのです。その方はひと目で私を気に入ってくれました。三歳の時です。うちは病院ですから、どのようになってもきちんと手当てをします、大事に育てますからといいます。　私をおいて帰り、駅に向かっているときに、母の考えが変わりました。　もう一度病院の家にひき返してきました。どんなに貧乏をしても、母子だから、やはり娘を離すことはできない、どんな苦労をしても自分で育てますので、一人で育てますので、いまの話はなかったことにしてください。

豊田郡に住んで農業をしていた祖母ナカを、広島に呼ぶことになりました。段原に家を借りて住み、母は看護婦として働いて、祖母が私の面倒をみることになりました。私は体が弱かったので、小学校には三学期になってはじめて通いました。でも、通知表は十点満点で、すべて八点、九点でした。　助役の伯父が私を可愛がり、よくみてくれていましたので勉強はすすんでいたのです。

二年にあがってから、伯父は広島駅から宮島駅に転勤することになりました。宮島は海も山もあり、空気がいいから、冬でも元気になるだろう、智佐子の体にいいからといって、

伯父夫婦と一緒に宮島に行くことになりました。

小学校は陸の方にもありましたが、船に乗るのがいいといわれ、厳島の小学校に一年間通うことになりました。移った宮島での生活で、たしかに体が丈夫になりました。厳島の古くからの旅館の子が級長で、宮島駅の助役の娘とみられていた私が副級長になりました。

そんな時代だったのです。

その後の一年間、三年生のときは、山口県の屋代島を目の前にする大畠に移りました。

伯父は一年ごとに転勤をくり返していたのです。こんどの学校は山の上にあります。そこにしか小学校がないのです。ここでの生活は毎日、歩いて、歩いて、体はだんだん丈夫になっていきます。国鉄の官舎の裏はすぐ海になります。鯛がよく獲れますし、子どもでも一時間ほどで、ギザミ（キョウセン）がバケツ一杯になります。私が町から転校してきたといってみな珍しがります。ほかの子の格好は、絣の着物に草鞋を履いて、前掛けをしています。私はワンピースを着て革靴を履いています。ランドセルを持っている都会の子なのです。

やはり駅の助役の娘さんだということで、ここでは級長になりました。いじめられることはまったくありません。家に帰るとすぐに友達がきて、私を海に連れていきます。泳ぎ

を覚えて大好きになったのは、この一年間のことでした。素潜りをする、遠泳もする、いちばん日焼けして頑丈になり、冬になっても風邪ひとつひかないようになっていました。その一年をすごして、小学校四年生からは己斐小学校に通うようになりました。己斐の町に住むようになってからは、母と祖母の三人で暮すようになりました。伯父は広島駅の駅長になる予定だったのですが、すでに中国との戦争の時代に入っておりました。急遽、上海の駅長として赴任していったのです。

戦争が終って、外地で戦っていた兵隊さんが続々と引き揚げてきました。祖母はもといた豊田郡に戻ることになりました。私は、己斐の家で母の治療をしながら働きました。岩国の手前、山口県との県境の近くに大竹町があります。そこに引揚援護局が設けられ、私はそこで働くようになりました。戦争に負けて、主に南方から兵隊さんが帰ってきます。みな一文無しで引き揚げてくるのですから、着いたらすぐ給料を渡さなければなりません。その援護局が、事務処理ができる人を募集していることを友達に教えられたのです。己斐の家の近くに裁縫を教える家があって、その裁縫の先生の姪にあたる娘が友達でした。二人で援護局で働くことにしました。

大竹引揚援護局は、大竹海兵団の跡地に設けられ、兵舎や格納庫が外地からの復員者・引揚者の宿舎、検疫所などにあてられました。建物の前庭にはゲートが造られ、右側に「御苦労様でした」、左側に「大竹引揚援護局職員一同」と大きな文字が書かれていました。

開局は昭和二十年十二月十四日。昭和二十二年二月二十一日の閉局までに、台湾、満洲、小笠原、沖縄、仏印・ビルマ、スマトラ、ボルネオ、ニューギニア、ソロモン・中部太平洋から四十一万人を超える引揚者を受け入れ、沖縄県人一一二七人を送出しております。

引揚者の兵隊さんはみな、船から上がってDDTを頭からかけられ、まっ白になって背嚢を担いできます。検疫を終えられ宿舎に入る前にすぐ名簿に署名してもらい、お金の入った袋が渡されます。

みな背嚢や水筒をたすきがけにして、命からがら上陸してくるのですが、なかにたった一人、背嚢もなにも持たずに、なにやら大事そうに抱えて、私の前に立たれた方がおりました。署名してもらうと、そこには「藤山一郎」とありました。なにも持たずにアコーディオンだけ、大事に抱えて日本に帰ってきたのです。「ああっ、藤山一郎さんですか！私たち憧れの方なんです。よくぞ、ご無事でお帰りになられて、ご苦労さまでした」と挨拶をしました。

56

　藤山一郎さんは、南方慰問団の一員として各地を回っておられましたが、ジャワ島で敗戦を迎え捕虜となり、のちにレバノン島に移され、昭和二十一年七月二十五日、復員輸送船となっていた航空母艦葛城に乗って大竹港に上陸されたのでした。

　援護局は、海兵団の宿舎に設けられましたので、大きな広間がありました。その晩は慰労会というのでしょうか、引き揚げてきたみなさんに集まってもらって、そこで藤山一郎さんが、抱えてきたアコーディオンを演奏し、歌ってくださいました。戦地のこと、戦友のことを思い出されたのでしょう、みなさん泣きながら聴き、いっしょに唄を歌っていました。戦死した人のこと、連れて帰ることができなかった人のこと、想いがつのって、みなさん泣かれるのです。

　この援護局で、私の夫となる竹岡清もいっしょに働いていました。竹岡は住んでいた向洋（なだ）から汽車に乗って大竹に向かう、途中の己斐から私も同じ汽車に乗ります。終戦すぐの汽車ですから乗客も少なく、いつもいっしょになるので話を交わすようになりました。「一度、家に遊びにきませんか」と誘われ、家にうかがうことにしました。

　あの日から一年も過ぎようという、夏のことです。家にうかがったとき、私は間違えて裏口から入って庭先に出てしまいました。そこでは、竹岡が下着一枚でハチマキをして七

57

輪を扇いでヤカンでお湯を沸かしていました。私がいるのに気づいて、じつに恥ずかしそうな顔をしたのをよく覚えております。あらためて玄関口に回りましたら、しばらくして、急いで着替えたのでしょう。夏場なのにきちんとした身なりで迎えてくれました。

「いま、お袋が買い物に行っとるんじゃ。帰ってきたらすぐにお茶を飲めるようにと思って、湯を沸かしとった」といいます。「ああっ、恥ずかしいところを見られた」という、その姿をみて、暑いなか、お母さんのことを思って湯を沸かして待っている、この人なら、私の母のことも大事にしてくれると思ったのです。

一年半ほど援護局に勤めているあいだに、こうして、竹岡と知り合いました。家族の方も、とてもいい方たちでした。長兄は中国電力に勤めておられ、次兄は日本精鉱所で秘書をしている方で、みな礼儀正しいおとなしい方たちでした。妹が二人おり、二人とも昭和女学校を卒業され、家族みな和気藹々とした家庭でした。私は兄妹もおりません、一人で育ってますので、家族が多いのがとても楽しかったのです。母のことも理解してくれて、いっしょに住んでくれるというので、竹岡と結婚することにしました。

私が玄関先で吹き飛ばされたあの家からすぐ近くに、新しく家を借りて、三人で生活をはじめました。終戦間もないころで、就職もむずかしい時代でした。夫は、しばらくは父

親がやっているアメリカ軍の請け負い仕事を手伝っていました。結婚して最初に生まれた赤ちゃんは色の白い、かわいい男の子でした。弘訓と名づけました。近所の人もやってきて、みんなで喜びました。このころには母の容態もだいぶよくなり、戦後の大混乱もようやくおさまってきそうで、あの生き地獄をくぐってきた私たちにも、かすかに希望を抱けるように思えました。

その日は寒い一月七日、朝から雪が降っていました。生まれて間もない弘訓が、ぎゅーっと手も足も縮めて苦しみはじめました。二時間前にはおっぱいもよく飲んでいたのに、まだ息をしているのにもう、口もこわばっておっぱいも飲むことができません。おかしい、どうしたんだろう。火の気も少ないので、赤ちゃんが凍えて死ぬかもしれない。早く助けなければと、近所のおばちゃんたちが、薪を持って集まってきました。お湯を沸かして助けようと、赤ちゃんを裸にして、びっくりしました。赤ちゃんの胸からおなかにかけて、私の腕に出ていた、あの薄紫色の斑点が、ずらーっと出ていました。生まれて十八日目のことで、ほどなくして亡くなりました。病名は「原爆症」、哀しい哀しい病名でした。

己斐国民学校は戦争が終ったのちも、何年も何年も私たちをさいなみ続けていました。かつての己斐国民学校は己斐小学校となったのですが、その小学校の校庭の土を入れ替えることに

なりました。雨が降るとグラウンドに水が溜まって運動会もできない。ところどころ緩くなっていて、子どもたちが大勢で一緒に走ると土が上下に動くのです。校庭は、被爆の二日後、事をしているときに、たくさんの人のお骨が掘り出されました。校庭は、被爆の二日後、二千人もの方の焼き場になったのですが、その一部がそのまま土を被せられて埋められていたのです。

知らせを受けた私たちは、遺骨を丁寧に弔う手伝いのために集まりました。お骨を拾って水できれいに洗い、新聞紙に包んで講堂のなかに並べるのです。大人のもの、子どものものと分けて並べていました。一人のお母さんが、その子どものお骨の前で涙を流しながらたたずんでいました。学校でお骨が見つかったと聞いてやってきた方でした。原爆で小学生の子どもを見失ってしまい、それから三年間、毎日写真を持って子どもを捜しつづけているといいます。小さな子どものお骨は、そのお母さんが貰い受けていきました。

父親の手伝いをつづけている夫を、長兄は心配してくれていました。軍の請け負いの仕事は忙しいうちはいいが、その波がひけたらどうするのか？ 心配してくれて、中国電力への就職をすすめてくれました。大会社の中国電力の職場には、どうやら縁故で就職した

方がたくさんいるようでした。みないい家庭の子弟なのですが、なぜかお酒を飲む方が多いのです。その人たちは、自分の給料を生活にあてる必要もあまりなく、自由に遣えるようなのです。夫はそうした上司に毎晩、毎晩誘われるようになりました。結婚したころは、お酒はほとんど飲めませんでした。わずかな量でも顔を赤くしてしまう、そんな人だったのですが。

二人目の男の子、誠治が生まれたときは、心配した症状はありませんでした。無事に育っていきました。下の女の子、真里子も無事に生まれました。でも、そのころにはもう、夫の酒が暴れだしていました。あまり飲めないといって断るのでしょうか、まあ、そう言わずにとなって、ずるずると。チャンポンというのでしょうか、ビールだ、次はウイスキー、お酒だとなって、毎晩、ぐでんぐでん、ふらふらになって帰ってきます。

また、人がいいうえに、根はおとなしい性格ですから、竹岡と飲めばあれが払ってくれるとなります。今日は早く帰らなければといっても、飲みに誘う人がいると断りきれない。こういうことになると、夫のいいところが全部、裏目裏目に出ていって、どんどん深まに嵌まっていきます。恐ろしいことです。当時は、給料も手渡しですから、ついには渡されたお金もどうなったか分からなくなるまで酔ってしまう。落としてしまったのか、盗と

61

ある日、近所の人がきて私に伝えます。お宅のご主人だと思うが、山の上の方の電信柱のところで眠っている人がいる、行ってみたらと教えてくれました。体裁は悪いし、恥ずかしいし、見にいきましたら、ぐでんぐでんに酔って、電信柱の元に弁当箱を枕にして、夫が寝ています。それが夜ならまだしも、まだ日の明るいうちで、もう、会社での仕事もさぼるようになったのです。その姿を見たら、情けないし、腹は立つはで。

そのうち夫は、苛立ちがつのって暴力を振るうようになりました。酒に飲まれて自分自身もなにがどうしてしまったのか、こんな筈じゃない、となって、自分に対する怒りを周りの者にぶつけるようになりました。夫の帰りは毎日御前様ですし、お金はない。母は原爆症で、私も身体が丈夫ではなくなっている。二人のまだ幼い子どもがいる。ほとほと困り果てました。

お風呂に入るにも、当時は主人がいちばんに入って、女の人はその後という固定観念が強かった時代ですから、夜中の一時過ぎ、二時近くなっても待っていなければなりません。ご飯だけは先に子どもにも、母にも食べさせていました。あるとき、夫が帰ってくるのも

られてしまったのか、なにしろ、給料袋には、ほとんどお金が入っていないのです。それが毎月のようになります。

62

だいたい二時になるからと、母を先に風呂に入れていたことがありました。間の悪いこと
にその時にかぎって少し早く帰ってきたのです。自分より先に風呂を使っているといって
怒りだし、風呂に入っている母を引きずり出して、投げ飛ばして、肋骨を折ったことがあ
りました。まだ保険もきちんとしていないころですので、母は医者にもかかることができ
ません。看護婦をしていた母にいわれて、あて木をしたり、湿布をしたりして直しました。

こうしたことがつづきました。二十四歳の私は、自殺を考えるようになりました。毎日、
毎日死ぬことを考えて暮らしていました。自分で死ぬといっても、首を吊っても、生き残っ
たらそれこそ恥になります。海に飛び込んで死のうかとも思いました。でも、私は泳ぎは
小さい時から上手ですから、思わず泳いでしまうでしょう。

鉄道自殺ならばと思いました。己斐駅と横川駅のちょうど中間に山手町があります。そ
こは大根畑で、当時は街灯もなにもなく。夜になると真っ暗になります。そこにほんの一
メートルくらい高くなった場所があり、一本松があります。夜中に汽車がピーポー、ピー
ポーと鳴らすことがあります。そのときは、一本松の付近で飛び込み自殺があるのです。「昨
日の夜、汽車がピーポー、鳴らしていたね。やはり自殺があったんだね」──「自殺場所」
と言われていました。

寒い、雪の降る夜でした。そこから飛び込もうと思って、女の赤ちゃんをおぶって、四歳になる男の子の手をひいて、一本松までとぼとぼと歩いていきました。横川駅を汽車が出るときに、ポーと鳴らしますので、どこまで汽車がきているのかが分かります。さあっ、いま飛び込もうとしたとき、背中の赤ん坊が、ギャーと泣きました。それで、はっとわれに返りました。そうだ、子どもを道連れにしてはいけない。いけないんだと自分に言い聞かせました。このときは、女の赤ちゃん、真里子が私の命を助けてくれました。

あの日から七年が経っていました。私は、半壊した水槽の中で抱きしめた、死んだ赤ちゃんの体の冷たさを思い出していました。あのときの怒りが、また込み上げてきました。子どもを道連れにして自分から死のうなんて、なんということを私は考えたのか。絶対にいけない。そんなことをしてはいけない。

原爆症が出るのではと心配した誠治は、小学校に入るようになりました。成績もよく、担任の先生が、「お宅ではどういう教育をなさっているのでしょう。よく勉強をしているようですが、塾に行かせているのでしょうか、ぜひ教えてください」とたずねてくるくらいでした。でも、教育もなにも、家にはその日のおかず代もないくらいですので、塾どこ

64

ろではありません。「家庭での教育はどのようにされていますか」と先生にいわれてもな

にも応えられずに、顔をまっかにして黙って耐えていました。近所の人は、父親が毎晩の

ように真夜中に酔い潰れて戻ってきて、暴れることを知っているのですから、なにもいえ

るわけがありません。

とうとうある日、夫の朝の出がけについ、私は言い出してしまいました。

「今日も遅く帰ると思うけど、子どものこともあるし、たまには早よ帰ったらどうな。こ

んな生活がずうーと続いたら、私が子どもの教育ができんようになる。学校では先生が、

家庭でよくしとられると思いますが、どういう風にされとりますか、言われても、私はひ

と言もなんにもいえん。ほじゃから、別れよう」

私から言い出しました。二人の子どもは私が引きとってなんとしても育てていきます。

あなたは中国電力に勤めているのですから、だれでも、お嫁さんのきてがあるから大丈夫

でしょう。中国電力は広島ではいちばんの会社で、給料も、ボーナスも退職金もいい職場

だったのですから。「じゃから、そうしよう。別れましょう」といいました。

それを聞いて夫は、会社にも行かず、酒を飲みはじめました。ウイスキーをラッパ飲み

し暴れはじめました。母はその朝、下の子をおんぶして市役所に行くためにもう家を出て

いました。夫は部屋中を壊して、私の髪の毛を摑んで引き回しました。髪を切られ、殴られ蹴られ、顔は腫れ上がり、痣だらけになりました。殴られ蹴られしながら、私は殺されてしまう、でももういい、と思っていました。夫の目を見ると、じつに哀しい目をしています。怒りというより、哀しい目なのです。

近所に聞こえてはならないと、私は声は出さずに堪えていたのですが、髪の毛を切られたとき、凄まじい痛みで、ついに「ギャー」と叫んでしまいました。家の前の道路をはさんで真向かいの散髪屋さんの奥さんが、悲鳴が聞こえたといって駆けつけてきました。きてみると、髪はばらばらに切られている、そこら中に血が飛び散っている、顔は腫れ上がっている。奥さんがびっくりして、「なにをしているのか、警察を呼びますよ！」と。

夫は出刃包丁を手にしていました。その包丁もよく切れるものならあまり痛くはないのですが、錆びついているものなのです。当時は、鉄くずを集めておくと買いにきてくれる人がいました。そうした物もおかず代の足しになるので、私が拾ってとっておいた包丁でした。その錆びついた包丁で髪を切られたのですから、もの凄い痛みになります。どうしても我慢ができなくなり、つい悲鳴を上げてしまったのです。

その日は、もう夏休みに入っていました。誠治は小学校の四年生でした。朝早く昆虫を

捕りに出かけたのですが、ちょうど帰ってきて裏から家に入ろうとして、この修羅場を見たのでしょう。誠治が私のところに駆け寄ってきて「お母ちゃん。早よ逃げなさい。ここに居ったら、本当に殺されてしまう」といって、私に五百円札を握らせます。どのようにして呼んだのか、表にタクシーを止めてあるという。私は、子どもに小遣いをあげたことはありませんでした。親戚の家に行ったときにいただいたのを貯めていたのか、分かりませんが、私に五百円札を握らせ、すぐに逃げなさいといいます。

そのとき、さあーっと、頭が静かになりました。そうだ、いまこの人に私が殺されたら、子どもたちは一生涯、苦しむことになる。人殺しの子どもとして生きていかなければならない。私は逃げなければいけない！　とっさに思って、表のタクシーに駆け込みました。

ひどい姿のままです。

逃げるといっても、私には兄妹もおりません。夫の妹が新天地で商売をしてましたので、そこに逃げました。妹も私の姿を見て、ひどく驚いて「お姉さん！　どうしたん」といって、傷を冷やして看病してくれました。その晩は妹のところに泊まりました。あくる日になって、ここしか行くところはないと、母と夫が迎えにきました。このときは、小学校四年生の誠治が、私の命を救ってくれました。

何回かあったのです。どうして、こんなことになってしまったのか！　言えば喧嘩にな
る、殴られる、暴力を振るわれる。酒に酔っての暴力は凄いものです。いつも、外にも出
られない姿になってしまいます。夫は毎日、毎日酔い潰れて戻ってくる。お金もない。子
どもの教育もできない。別れようといっても別れることができない。もう、本当にこの人
が死んでくれればいい、とさえ思うようになってしまいました。それくらい苦しみました。

その年の大晦日、十二月三十一日に夫が交通事故を起こしました。すぐ近くに派出所が
あり、「もう、息がない」と伝えてきました。体を包むために毛布を持って、五日市の病
院に行ってくださいという。お金もないので、タクシーで行くこともできません。夫の妹
のところには車も電話もありましたので、派出所から電話をしてもらいました。車を回し
てもらい、病院に着くと、夫がちょうどレントゲンを撮り終えて出てきたところでした。

死なないでいてくれたのですが、それも嬉しいことではなくなっていました。私は、人間
の心を失いかけていたのです。　形を変えたあの「生き地獄」の続きでした。

三
希
望

お酒に振りまわされている夫と、別れるにも別れられず、死ぬにも死ねない。そんな日々をくり返しながら、昭和三十四年（一九五九年）に入っていました。私の窮状を見かねて、近所の奥さんが通ってくるようになりました。小学校の先生をしておられたご主人を原爆で亡くされた、泉広さんという常識の豊かな婦人でした。創価学会員でした。家にくる度に、当時『大白蓮華』に連載されていた、湊邦三さんの「小説　日蓮大聖人」を読んでください。

「この日蓮大聖人のことは、小説の形をとっていますが、つくりごとではありません。事実あった歴史ですから。絶対に迷うことはないですよ。願いとして叶わざるはなしのご本尊さまです。あなたがいま、変わらなければ、いつ変わるのですか」と、私に、創価学会の信心をすすめてくれます。

それまでに、私はさまざまな宗教に迷っていました。でも、どこかに真実をとらえている宗教があるのではと求めていました。なんとかして助かりたいと願って、天理教、立正

70

佼成会、黒住教、と話を聴きに行きましたが、どこに行っても、納得できるものではありませんでした。作り話としか思えないし、なにかこころに染み込むことがない。己斐駅の近くにある、キリスト教の教会にもいってみたのですが、これがいちばん、ばかげた話としか思えませんでした。

泉広さんの筋のとおった明快な話をきいているうちに、これは本物に違いない、この信心をしてみようという気持ちが、私のなかに湧き上がってきました。「私にできるかね」とたずねると、「できますよ。自分が変わることによって、不幸な人が幸福になり、幸福な人がますます幸福になる、すごい信心ですよ」といいます。

じつはこの五年前、昭和二十九年に母が創価学会の信心をはじめていました。やはり、母と同年代の泉広さんのすすめによるものでした。重い原爆症を抱える母は、自分の命を変えるのだといって、信心をつづけていました。

小学生になっていた誠治が「おばあちゃん、ぼくが南無妙法蓮華経って唱えれば、うれしいかね」「そりゃ、誠坊さんが唱えてくれればうれしいよ」といったやりとりを、母としていたのも知っていました。誠治は家を出る時と帰った時に二階の母の部屋に行き、題目を三唱するようになっていました。テストを先生から受け取ると二階に上がって題目を

唱える、通知表をもらうと二階に行って題目を唱えるのです。座談会に行くときも、母は子どもたちを連れて参加していました。

こうして子どもたちは信心を実践していたのですが、夫は大反対でした。母の部屋で座談会をするときがありました。すぐに夫は下の部屋で大音量でレコードをかけ、じゃまをします。「今日、会社から帰ってくるまでに、そのご本尊とやらをなくしておけ！」と母を怒鳴りつけることもありました。こうしたなかでは、私一人だけが信心をはじめるわけにはいきません。私一人がはじめれば、それがまた喧嘩の種になりますし、夫はますます、独りになってしまいます。私は髪を切られたときの、夫の哀しい目が忘れられないでいました。どうにかして、夫と「いっしょに」信心をはじめられないかと願っていました。

このころ、夫はいったん会社に出ても、すぐ席をはずしていなくなってしまうようになっていました。ある日、私は会社に呼ばれました。示しがつかないといわれました。当時の中国電力では社員を解雇することはめったにないのですが、どうにも示しがつかない、会社を辞めてもらえないかというのです。

「竹岡さんは、仕事をしない。すぐにいなくなるんじゃ。どこに行ったか捜すと、近くの喫茶店でコーヒーを飲みよるか、映画館に入って寝とる。どうにもならん。子どもさんが

72

二人おられるから、たいへん気の毒だとは思うんじゃけど、会社を辞めてもらわんといけんような状態になりました」

そのとき私は、もう信心をはじめなければいけないと心に決めました。近くに住む大工さんで、創価学会の班長さんをしている増井さんに家にきてもらい。二人でいっしょに信心をはじめようと、夫と話をしました。

「そんならなにか。わしゃ、飲み屋にいっぱい借金があるんじゃ。信心したら、この借金なくなるんかい」

「なくなります。　間違いありません」

「ほんじゃ、だんだん、酒もやめられるようになるかい」

「なります。　願いとして叶わざるはなしです。なんでも真剣に祈って実践すれば、願っているとおりになります」

「ほおー、ならんかったら、どうするんかい！」

「ならんかったら、どげんでも、あなたの思うようにしてください」

「わしゃ、いま会社をクビになりそうなんじゃ。クビにならんようになるかい」

「なります。その代わり、約束してください。きちんと朝晩の勤行をして、折伏行に励ん

73

でください。やはり、することをしなきゃ仏さまの力もありません」

自分でなにもしないで、することをしなきゃ仏さまの力もありません」

めるのは間違っている。そういう生き方を「外道」というんです。お酒に溺れてしまった

ことも、飲めない者に酒をすすめ誘惑した、上司やお仲間が悪いと思っておいででしょう。

でも、違いますよ。原因は自分のなかにあるんじゃないですか。誘惑の種ならまわりにい

くらでも渦巻いているじゃないですか。——班長さんは懇々と話をしてくれました。それ

をじっーと聞いていた夫は「ほじゃ、やってみよう」といいました。その言葉を聞いたと

き、胸がぱあーっと暖かくなり、体が軽くなったのを覚えております。私たち二人はその

日にすぐ、創価学会に入会しました。

その増井班長さんはすごい人でした。次の日から毎日、大工の仕事を終えてから夕方六

時前に家にきて題目を唱えながら夫を待ちます。約束したことは守る人ですから、夫も六

時には帰宅して、いっしょに勤行をします。勤行を終えると二人で折伏行に出かけるので

す。毎晩、毎晩これを続けたおかげで、夫はどんどん変わっていきました。なにかが動き

はじめました。昭和三十四年十一月のことです。あの日から、十四年が経っていました。

夫は給料袋もきちんと持って帰るようになり、お酒を飲むのもだんだん少なくなっていきました。事務処理の能力に長けていることが分かって、学会活動後の書類の整理に携わるようになりました。毎晩帰宅は一時、二時になります。前と同じ時間なのですが、かつては酒に酔いしれて、ふらふらしながら帰ってきました。いまは、自転車をこいで元気に戻ってきます。

ある日私は、支部の角屋婦人部長さんに呼ばれました。お宅のご主人が帰宅するのは、毎晩一時、二時でしょう、心配されていると思います。今晩、九時に家にいらっしゃい。なにをされているか分かりますから。毎日統監の処理をしているのは、白島にある、福島さんというお宅でした。夫は、じつに熱心に書類の整理をしておりました。

「見てご覧なさい。帰宅が遅くなるのは、ああして、創価学会のために、みんなのために一所懸命やっておられるのですから。安心してください」

夫は、折伏行が大好きになりました。ほどなくして、組長、班長、地区部長となり、二人で己斐支部の支部長、婦人部長を任せられるようになりました。当時の創価学会の中国地方の拠点は岡山にありました。岡山から中心者が広島にきて、幹部会が開かれたとき、私も夫といっしょに参加しました。このときは、午前二時まで会合が行われました。一人

ひとり、支部の折伏の状況、目標をきかれるのです。みんな十人、二十人と応えるのですが、眼から火が出るくらいに叱られます。

「十人、二十人の折伏で世界の民が救えるか！　広宣流布ができると思うのか！　なにをたわけたことをゆうとるのか！」

そして、夫を見ています。「おい、電気屋」。夫が中国電力に勤めていることは知っておりますから、こう呼ばれておりました。

「おい、電気屋。お前んとこは、なんぼするのかね」

「はい！　百人やります」

「百人？　できんかったら、どうするかね」

「できんかったら、ぼうずになります！」

それから、夫も私も、支部全体、折伏、折伏と必死に活動しました。親戚、知り合いはもとより、橋の下に住んで物乞いをしている人にも、信心をすすめました。当然のことでした。あの、どこにも出口のなかったときから三年、夫も私も実際に人生を変えることができたのですから、どんな状況にある人でも信心の話をしました。その方も入会されてから生活をあらため、仕事にも就き、組織では支部長をされ、市会議員になりました。この

76

とき己斐支部全体で九十九人が新たに入会しました。一人足りません。夫は坊主頭になりました。顔は日に焼けて黒いのですが、頭だけ真っ青になっています。いま思いだしても、その姿がおかしくて、おかしくて。

学会活動に励んでいた夫は、この間、中国電力の労働組合の委員長を頼まれるようになりました。学会活動で目標をもつことにより、職場でもかなり積極的に仕事をし、発言するようになっていたのです。そして、根がやさしい人ですから、面倒見のよいところを期待されたのだと思います。夫のいい性格が今度は、いい方向、いい方向に回転していったのです。学会の幹部の方に指導を受けたところ、「大事なことですから、いいじゃないですか、引き受けなさい」といわれ、組合の活動もすることになりました。この委員長時代もはさんで、夫は最終的に三十八年間、中国電力に勤務して、定年になるまで勤め上げることができました。

創価学会の活動をはじめて一家に功徳の華が咲くようになって、私も自分のしたいことができるようになってきました。なにかしたい、世の中のためになにかしたいという思いが強く湧いてきました。

女学校に入る前のことが思いおこされます。己斐の町で、母と祖母と、三人で暮らすようになったころ、私は自分の父親はどういう人なのかを知りたくなってきました。母にはたずねにくいので、祖母に聞きました。「あんたの父親は、岡山の方におられる立派なお医者さんじゃ」——なにも心配せずに、あなたはしっかり勉強していればいい、いずれ入籍もしてくれるから心配することはないと聞かされました。そのとき私は、では女医になろうと決心しました。

広島でも一、二を争う山中高等女学校に進学しました。百年以上の歴史をもつ学校です。情緒豊かな、勉強も裁縫も、なんでもできる、中流以上の生活をしている娘しかとらないところです。そこで勉強して、女医になるために医学部のある岡山大学にすすもうと決めていました。

女学校の二年の時に、敵性語だといって英語が廃止になりました。学校に行っても、お弁当を持って、すぐに被服廠や兵器廠にかりだされます。学業も中途半端のまま、「卒業」になりました。のちには女子挺身隊に編入されて兵器の部品を作る工場で働きましたので、私の夢は、戦争で全部だいなしになっていました。

土居の父は、昭和三十九年（一九六四年）十二月十三日に亡くなりました。悲しいことに、母は家の外らせを受けて、母と二人で忠海の土居家に急いで行きました。父の死の知

で待つことになり、私だけが父の枕元に通されました。枕元にはシキミが立てられていました。以前、主人と二人で父を折伏にいき、日蓮大聖人の御書をとおして仏法の話をしました。父はお題目をあげることを約束してくれました。こうしたことが二度、三度ありましたので、その意を汲んでくれたのでしょう。

私はそっと顔にかかった白布をあげました。なんとその顔の美しいこと。半眼半口、うっすらと笑みを浮かべているような口先。半眼はじっと私を凝視めており、その眼がキラリと光りました。

「あっ、義眼だ」

若きころ愛し合った母の右眼は、被爆によって失われ、義眼になっていました。父は、母にも娘にも何もしてあげられなかった、その最後の想いを、自分の義眼にたくし私たちに伝えたかったのでしょうか。父の両眼は、若い学生さんに捧げられたのでした。医者としての本分を果たしたのだと思いました。

そして今、父と母、生まれて十八日で亡くなった長男の三人は、静かに静かに、あの広大な広島平和記念墓苑で、幸せに眠っています。

私は父と同じように医者になりたいと思っていましたが、戦争の混乱によって女医にな

ることは叶いませんでした。それでは、「先生」の名がつくものをしたいと思いました。

まずは、編み物の先生を目指しました。最初は富士編み機の学校、そしてブラザーに通って編み物の勉強に励みました。編み物の国家試験を受けていたのですが、創価学会の信心をはじめた翌年、その結果が昭和三十五年の四月に届き、資格をえることができました。

すぐに己斐上町で編み物教室を開いて、生徒さんをとるようになりました。一人とても熱心な生徒さんがいたので、その方も資格をとれるようにしました。その方は、現在も己斐上町で教室を開いております。

そのころ、文章を書いて雑誌の懸賞に応募したことがあります。当時発刊されていた婦人誌のうち私は『主婦の友』を読んでおりました。秋山ちえ子さんの社会探訪や、曾野綾子さんによる女性の手紙の指導、手芸の欄も充実しており、小説も、井上靖さん、佐多稲子さん、司馬遼太郎さんの連載がありました。この雑誌で、愛情のすばらしさを綴った「愛の記録」の募集をしておりました。賞金は二十万円とありました。私は、夫と結婚してから危機を乗り越えるまでの過程を、原稿用紙五十枚ほどにまとめました。「みだれ髪」と題をつけました。

信心のことをうまく文章に盛り込めなかったのは残念でしたが、このころには、あの凄

80

まじい生活の意味を文章に綴ることができるくらい、心の余裕が生まれていたのです。昭和三十七年の新年号に、入選作の発表がありました。六百篇を超える応募があり、三人の方の作品が入選作に選ばれました。掲載された「太陽は再び没せず」を書かれた旭川市の林田律子さんは、のちの三浦綾子さん。二年後に『氷点』で有名になられた方です。このとき私は次点になりましたので、水色のきれいな毛糸を一ポンド贈っていただきました。大人のセーター二枚は編める量です。二人の子どものためにセーターを編んでやりました。セーターを編みながら、まだ私には、なにかができる、きっとできると感じていました。

誠治は修道中学・高校に進学しました。家にお金の余裕はありませんでしたから、毎日、自転車で通学させ、夏休みも、冬休みも弁当を持たせて学校に行かせました。家庭教師をつけることはできませんので、学校に行って毎日図書館で勉強しなさいと教えました。図書館にいけば上級生もいますので、分からないところは上級生に教えてもらいなさい。教員室にいけば先生もいる。その日に学習したことは、その日に頭のなかに入れて覚えなさい、といつも諭しておりました。明日にまわすのは絶対にいけないと、言い聞かせていました。

誠治が高校三年にあがったとき、己斐駅の近くでクリーニング店を開くことになりました。学会の班長さんで、クリーニング店をいとなんでいる方がおりました。本店と支店の二店を経営していました。ある日、相談にきました。親が病気になり、大きなお金が必要なので一店、店を買ってくれないかという。まだまだ私たちは貧乏の最中で、十円のお金でさえ大事にしていたときです。三百万円で買ってくれないかという。幹部の方に指導をうけたところ、親を大事に思っていっているのだから、買ってやってもいいじゃないか。仕事はあなたはできないだろうが、いまの店の職人さんをそのまま雇ってつづければ大丈夫だろうといいます。

どうしたら三百万円の都合がつけられるかと考え、とうとう夫の父親のところに行きました。誠治が大学に進学するのにお金がいる、と説明しました。他人に渡すのでは話を聞いてくれるわけもありませんから、嘘をついてしまいました。それならと、父は、住んでいる家の土地を担保にするから銀行から借りなさいという。担保は父の土地ですが、私の名義で銀行から三百万円を借りました。

三百万円を借りると、五十万円は銀行の口座に残しておかなければなりません。二百五十万円の現金を下ろして、これでお父さんを入院させて、早く元気にさせてあげてくださ

いと渡したその晩、その班長さんは夫婦二人して、何処かへ身を隠してしまいました。ま
だお店の権利の手続きも済ませておりません。大きな借金が残ってしまいました。
　クリーニング店の隣りで散髪店をしていた人が、逃げた人の弟でした。この方が誠実な
やさしい方でした。——兄がいなくなってから本店も、この隣りの店もだれもいなくなっ
ている。「店の権利の件も、私がきちんとさせるから、竹岡さん、この店をやってください」
というのです。
　夫は中国電力の社員ですから、他の職業をもつわけにはいきません。散髪店さんの弟さ
んに証人になってもらい、お店の名義をすぐ私にきりかえたのですが、私にはクリーニン
グの技術もなにもありません。支部婦人部長をしているときです。すべてを学会活動にあ
てていますので、その職人さんを頼り、信用して任せる以外になかったのです。三か月ほ
ど経って、まず問屋から「お店からの支払いが、もう何か月もありません」といってきま
した。職人さんが売り上げを自分のものにしてしまい、支払いをしていないのです。この
処理がたいへんでした。
　店は己斐駅のすぐ近くにあります。夏のある日、店に行ってみますと、ひと目でその筋
の者と分かる男の人が、店の前に立っています。刺青を見せびらかすようにして私にいい

ました。「あんたかね、この店を乗っ取ったのは!」

逃げた人に、店を担保にお金を貸しているという。だから、店はその者たちのものだというのです。大きな声を張り上げて、威嚇してくるのです。まわりの方たちも、なにが起こったのかと集まってきましたので、家で話をきくことにしました。ここでは人の迷惑になるからと、店を閉めて家に向かいました。己斐上町まで連れていって、家に上がってもらいました。すると、一階の八畳間にある仏壇を見て、たずねてきました。

「お宅は、学会ですか?」

そうですよと応えると、「役職は、奥さん、なにですか」とききます。私は支部婦人部長ですよというと、「へえー、申し訳ありません!」と手を突いて謝ります。どうやら、店に目をつけたこちらの者から雇われて、大阪からきたようでした。「申し訳ありません! もう二度と、私のような者がくるようにはさせませんので」といって帰りました。家には私一人しかおりませんし、心のなかでは恐ろしいばかりで、とうとう名前も聞きませんでした。少し前に、京都や大阪のそうした方で若い者をみんな折伏し、更生させている人が、何人かいるとは聞いていましたが、家にきた人もそうした方の一人だったのでしょうか。

84

お店で雇っている職人さんには、辞めてもらわなければならないのですが、なかなか言い出せないでいました。この問題を解決しようと、一所懸命にお題目をあげていました。

ある日お客さんが、「お店でクリーニングしてもらった服が、切れてしまっている」と持ってきました。見るとコートの後ろが、上から三分の一くらい裂けてしまっています。職人さんを呼んで、これはあなたの仕事ですかと見せると「へぇ、あっしがやりました」といいます。「お客さんの物だから、これじゃ弁償せないけんが」。すると、大声で「わしゃ、弁償はようせんよ！」といって、それきり店にこなくなりました。守られました。どんなに本人が悪いといっても、辞めてもらうにはお金がいりますし、恨みに思われることもありますから。

数日後、広島市でいちばん古くからクリーニング店を営んでいる方が、私をたずねてきました。はじめてお会いする方でしたが、私がお店のことで困っていることを知って、応援してあげようと思ったといいます。学会員の方でした。創価学会の座談会では、家庭のこと、病気の悩み、仕事のこと、なんでも語ってみなで励ましあっていましたから、私が座談会で話したことを、どこからか伝え聞いたのでしょう。

その方に、クリーニング店のそれまでのいきさつ、私に技術がなく任せられる職人さん

もいないこと、などを聞いてもらいました。お店の設備をすべて確認して、その方が――

奥さん、これなら大丈夫ですよ。私が教えてあげますから、奥さん自分でやりなさい、といいます。丁寧にきちんと仕事をすれば、これなら収益も上がる筈ですから、お金もほどなく返せるでしょう、人を雇わないで自分でやりなさいというのです。

次の日から、活動を終えて夜九時になると、その方が店にみえて、アイロンのかけ方、しみ抜きの仕方、どうやってきれいに洗い干すのか、器械の使い方、衣服の素材についての知識などをすべて教えてくださいました。店には古くはなっていましたが、広島でも数台しかないといういい器械があることも知りました。仕事をする設備はすべて整っていました。お金を持って逃げてしまった班長さんも、私たちを騙すつもりはなかったことが分かりました。

技術を学んで、一人でクリーニング店をはじめた私は、朝早くから店を開け、夕方七時には店を閉め学会活動をつづけました。幹部の方に報告し指導を受けましたら、「店のほうも、しっかり頑張りなさい」と激励をしてくださり、私をサポートする副婦人部長を、すぐに決めてくれました。仕事をはじめると、近くにも二、三クリーニング店がありましたが、一人では手に余るくらいのお客さんがみえるようになりました。

86

広島カープの山本浩二さんもお客さんの一人でした。シャツは手洗いできちんとアイロンをかけたのがいい、今度はテレビに出るからといって、いつもお店の前に車を止めて入ってきます。そのうちに若い人が目に見えて多くくるようになりました。話ししやすいのかどうか、若い人たちはいろいろな相談ごとを持ち込んできます。仕事と若い人たちの相談相手で夕方七時まで、大忙しの毎日になりました。

私たちが信心をはじめ、夫が変わっていくのを見ていちばん喜んだのは母でした。

終戦直後、母の体は痩せにやせて衰弱しており、もう死んでしまうかと嘆いていたときに、岡山の陸軍病院が機能していることを伝え聞きました。すぐに連絡をとって入院させてもらい、母は岡山で一か月半の治療を受けることができました。ようやく命をとりとめた状態でした。しかし、重度の原爆症で体力はなく、右半身のケロイドが冬になると痛みだすことが何年かつづきました。その容態は、ゆっくりとよくなっていきました。

母は病院には通っていましたが、このころ近所の人たちは、軽い病気のときは病院に行くより母に診てもらうのがいいと、母を頼りに家にやってきていました。また、注射をしてもらいにきていました。まだまだお金も少ない時代ですので、薬局にいって、カルシウ

87

ムやビタミンを買って母のところにきます。家から動けない方のところには、母のほうから出向いて診てやっておりました。

自分の容態も、まだ寝たり起きたりのときでしたが、婦長をしていたときからの使命感というのでしょうか。人を助けることで、自分自身も生きる力がつづいていったのだと思います。

被爆してから三年、母が顔の中央、鼻のつけ根がかゆいといって、かきむしります。血が出るほどかいていると、そこから三角形の小さいガラスが出てきました。残っていたのです。母の鼻は上と下の二箇所が折れていましたので、折れた上の骨の下にガラスが入り込んでいたのでしょう、三年かかって出てきたのです。

一家でいちばん最初に信心をはじめ、唱題に励むようになってから、母は子どもたちのことをよくみてくれておりました。夫の給料がほとんど飲み代に消えていた時期は、私の手伝い仕事の収入で生活が支えられていましたので、子どもたちの世話は母に頼るしかありませんでした。その間に、母は孫たちに題目を唱えることの大切さを、教えてくれていたのです。

母は、昭和四十二年（一九六七年）二月二十八日に、胃がんで亡くなりました。原爆症

88

を抱えながら、命を二十二年間永らえたのです。その前に、誠治は中央大学合格の報告をしていました。母は「誠治の願うとおりにしてやりなさい」と言い残して、喜びに満ちて亡くなっていきました。

四　共戦

宿命を使命にかえて

四十歳代になった私は、朝から店に出て、食事もゆっくりとれないくらいクリーニング店で働いていました。仕事は山とあります。着古した作業着を身に着け、次から次へと服の素材を確認し仕分けして洗い、体重をのせて重いアイロンをかけます。すでに比治山学園の中学生になっていた娘、真里子が私が仕事をしている姿を見て「ああっ、お母ちゃん、そんな姿をして仕事をするんか！　可哀そうに！　おばあちゃんが生きとって見たら、泣くよ」といいますが、やめるわけにはいきません。

　二人の子どもを連れて汽車に飛び込もうとしたとき、赤ちゃんだったこの娘、真里子が背中で大声で泣いて、二十四歳の私を思い止まらせてくれました。誠治は小学校四年生のとき、私の命を父親から救ってくれました。その二人に母が信心を教え、私たちも創価学会に入会しました。生活を立て直し人生を変えることができ、生きることの豊かさを知ることができました。　私たちは、子どもたちには、きちんとした教育を授けようと、懸命に働いてきました。

92

修道高校を卒業し中央大学に合格した誠治は、母が亡くなってすぐ、東京へと向かいました。私を育ててくれた大事な大事な母と、一切の希望を託していた息子の二人を、私は同時に失いました。広島大学に入っていっしょに生活してほしいと思っていましたが、母が最後に「誠治の願うとおりにしてやりなさい」と言い遺していたのです。

「池田先生にさしあげるから、もう、広島に帰ってこんでええ」といって、東京に送り出したものの、私は身体の半分をもがれたように、寂しく切ない思いをしていました。毎日、己斐上町の家の二階から、誠治が修道高校から自転車で戻ってくる坂道をみつめていました。そんな私を見て、夫は「もう、いいかげんにせんか！」といって叱ります。一年のあいだ、私はふと気づくと二階の誠治の部屋から海の方へつづく坂道を見ていました。そんな思いを、忙しいクリーニング店の仕事が紛らしてくれていました。

クリーニング店はその後、三十数年つづけることになります。三百万円は数年で返済しましたので、生活の支えのためということはもうありませんでした。しかし、私は器械も新しく入れ替えて、店の内装も構えもきれいに直して、お店をつづけました。途中からは手伝いの人にもきてもらいましたが、七十歳代まで、体力的に無理かなとなるまでお店をつづけました。もう仕事をやめなければと思っていたころに、店舗を私に貸していた大家

さんのほうから申し出がありました。建物をビルに建て替えなければならないので、といって立ち退き料まで払ってくれました。

仕事をつづけて数年して、私は婦人たちの全国組織、「主婦同盟」の広島の議長、責任者になりました。十五年間つづく活動がはじまりました。私が現在のように、みなさんに被爆の体験を語る平和活動をつづけているのは、この主婦同盟の運動がきっかけとなりました。

主婦同盟の全国の議長会は年に二回あり、そこで各県の活動内容の報告が行われます。名古屋ではじめられた「けちけち運動」でした。名古屋での運動を、発行されていた「主婦同盟ニュース」で知り、まず公共料金を毎月いくらぐらい使っているかを調べました。領収書を持って集まり、水道代、電気代、電話代を比べてみると、なかに水道代に四万円かかっている方がいます。夫婦に子どもが二人の四人でです。商売を営んでいる家でもありません。みなは三千円ほどで、よく使う人でも五千円です。聞いてみると、洗濯をするときに、水を出しっぱなしにしていました。それを改めてみると、やはり、三千円ほどで済むようになりました。

私たちの運動は、私たち自身の生活スタイルを見直し、改革していくことがテーマでした。どんなに物が豊かになり、便利な世の中になっても、家庭を守る主婦が、かしこい生活を見いだしていかなければ、社会の根底がゆらいでしまうからです。次に調べたのは、牛乳でした。これは私が大好きだったこともありますが、子どもたちに飲ませることが多いので日頃から気にかかっていたのです。

私たち一家が懇意にしている、牧場を経営している知人からいただく牛乳はとても濃く、味わいも深いのですが、町で売られている牛乳はかなり薄いと思っていました。みなで手分けして、広島で売られているすべての牛乳を持ち寄って飲み比べてみました。濃い、中くらい、水っぽいと分けて、いちばん薄い牛乳を生産している工場まででかけました。見学させていただくと、やはり製造の工程が、どうもおかしいことが分かります。調べに行ったのは、公表するためではありません。公表すれば、ご商売の妨害をすることになってしまいます。私たちの運動は、私たち自身の生活改革ですので、このことを知った私たちだけは、その製品を買わないようにしよう、いい牛乳を製造しているところのものを買うようにして、応援しましょうと決めました。

次に、私たちが毎日のようによく食べる、お豆腐を調べました。お願いして朝四時ごろ

に何軒かのお店に行きました。たくさん積んである大豆はどこで収穫されたものなのかをうかがうと、アメリカから仕入れているというお店がありました。これは気をつけないといけないと思いました。当時、アメリカでは広大な農場で、飛行機で農薬を撒いていることが報じられていましたので、輸入食糧のことが気にかかっていました。

別府の高崎山のニホンザルに奇形が生じているのは、餌にしている輸入食糧の影響ではないかと疑われていることを知り、みなで高崎山に行きました。腰が立たないサルや手が半分失われているサルがたくさんいるのを見て、やはりあのお店の豆腐は買わないようにしようと決めました。

当時、広島の大根は一本二百円くらいで売られていました。なぜこんなに高いのか？では、近在の大根をつくっている農家から直接仕入れようと思い、数人で軽トラックで買い付けに行きました。漬物用にまとめて買って、みなで分けようと話しあったのです。値段を聞いてもなかなか返事が返ってきません。なんで値段をすぐ決められないのだろう？　やっと値段が決まって聞いて驚きました。市販の値段とまったく変わりません。流通経路を調べてみました。広島でつくられた大根は、いったん大阪に運ばれ、大阪の市場で値段をつけられ、また広島に運ばれ店で売られていることを知りました。

主婦にとっては大問題でしたので、このことだけは、公明党の議員の方に知らせて対処してもらうことにしました。農協と折衝して、大阪で値をつけることをやめさせてくださいと訴えました。庶民がいちばんよく使う食材でこんなことをされては、困るからです。

ほどなくして、大根の値段は下がりました。大阪に運ぶことはなくなりました。

こうした主婦同盟の運動で明らかになった私たちの社会が抱える課題は、その後に大きな社会問題として浮かび上がっていきました。私たちは昭和五十年代の初期から、すでに高齢化社会を見すえて、主婦としてどう対処していくかを考え、一人ひとりの運動をすすめていました。全国各県で、かしこい生活をするためのあらゆる運動を行って、主婦同盟は平成二年（一九九〇年）に十五年間の活動を終えました。

国連で初の軍縮特別総会が開かれたのは、戦争が終って三十数年も経た、昭和五十三年（一九七八年）五月のことでした。この時、創価学会第三代会長の池田大作先生は国連軍縮特別総会を前に、ワルトハイム国連事務総長あてに、核軍縮および核廃絶のための十項目を提唱された書簡を送っております。

その四日前の五月二十日、池田先生は広島の地で本部幹部会を開催してくれました。広

島文化会館をたたれた池田先生が岡山に向かうことを告げられた私たち一家は、感謝の思いで池田先生をお見送りしようと、広島駅に向かいました。思いだしても胸が熱くなって、短くは纏められませんので、当時の日記を記させていただきます。

「池田先生が広島文化会館においでになっていることを聞きました。どうか池田先生が御無事で広島をたたれるようにと、朝から題目をあげていました。主人、真里さん、私の三人で車に乗り、すぐ広島駅に行きました。しばらくすると、森田副会長、上田副会長、徳野副会長とともに、先生のお姿が拝せられました。真里さんと、私と、（女子部の）板垣さんは、じっと先生の方を見つめました。先生はふとこちらを御覧になり、二、三歩近づいて『お世話になりました。どうぞお元気で』と声をかけてくださったのです。ひと目だけ、先生のお元気な姿を遠くから拝するだけでよいと思っておりましたのに、慈悲の言葉をおかけいただいて、私たちは胸が一杯でした。

さらに、あとから来た主人はプラットホームに出て、上田副会長より先生に紹介されたそうです。『竹岡さんのお父さんですね。知ってますよ。私と一緒に岡山にいらっしゃい。すぐこの列車に乗りなさい。キップを手配しなさい』とおっしゃってくださったそうです。

私たちは別なところにいたので、同じ列車に間に合わず、次の新幹線で、岡山文化会館に

行きました。

ちゃんと手はずを整えてくださって、上田副会長は『今日はみなで会食ですよ。三人とも池田先生が招待してくださったのです』とおっしゃってくださり、大広間に通してくださり、一番前で親子三人、大鍋の御馳走をいただきました。池田先生は大広間に『今日は！』といって入ってこられ、一番に私たちのところにおいでになって、『お父さん、来てましたか、よかったですね』とおっしゃってくださり、主人のすぐ前にお座りになり、題目三唱されました。なんともったいないこと、なんと嬉しいこと。夢ではないやら。私たちは先生の真心の、そして岡山の皆さんの心よりの労苦を感謝しながら、素晴らしい御馳走をいただきました。

その間、先生はずうっと一人ひとりの方々を激励され、また指導されながら食事をされました。本当に先生は、一人の人を、どんなに大切にされ、どんなに慈しまれ、どんなに激励され、本当に心の休まる時もなく、対話されておられます。

そのお姿に接して、私たちもより一層、広布に役立つ人間にならねばならぬことを、心に誓いました。池田先生、ありがとうございました。昭和五十三年五月二十一日」

会食ではありましたが、池田先生は参加者一人ひとりの激励のため、料理に箸をつける

時間もほとんどありません。終了後、さらに池田先生は私たち三人を、香川の庵治研修道場にまで招待してくださいました。

岡山から宇野へ移動し、宇野港から小型のクルーザーに乗船して研修道場に向かいます。

私たちの乗った船には池田先生の御次男も乗船しておられてから、もうすぐ夕暮れを迎える素晴らしい瀬戸内海を眺めていたとき、池田先生が来られて夫に、「きれいな海ですから、ゆっくり泳いでいきなさい」と声をかけました。朝広島駅に向かったときは、こんなことになるとは思いもよりません。何の用意もありませんので、夫はパンツ一枚で庵治の海を満喫しておりました。そこへ小船に乗った池田先生が近寄り、「ああ、お父さん、竹岡さん。ここでは美味しい貝が、サザエが獲れますから、味わってくださいね」とまた声をかけられます。これを聞いた地元の漁業関係の方が海に潜って、サザエを私たちのために三ツ、四ツ、獲ってくださいました。

三十数年を経た今でも、このときの光景が鮮明に浮かんできます。竹岡家にとって忘れられない思い出です。娘の真里子も「あの日があったから、その後の三十数年、私たち一家は純粋に信心に励み、歩んでこれたのだ」と述懐しております。

昭和五十四年（一九七九年）四月二十四日、ラジオのニュースで池田先生が第三代会長

100

を退き名誉会長になられることを知りました。突然のことでした。池田先生がどうして！心が乱れました。翌二十五日の聖教新聞に「全国会員の皆様へ」という挨拶が掲載されましたが、どうしても理解できません、納得がいきません。いったい、なにが起こっているのか、私たちにはまったく分かりませんでした。五月三日には「七つの鐘」総仕上げ記念と銘打たれた第四十回本部総会が東京八王子の創価大学体育館で行われましたが、そのときは拍手もほとんどすることなく、創価学会の会合でいままで見たこともない重苦しく、なんとも言えない暗い会合だったと、総会に出席した方からうかがいました。

それから一年間、池田先生のことは聖教新聞で報じられることも、いっさいなくなりました。どこにも、一行たりとも載っていないのです。それは寂しい一年間でした。いままで楽しくて楽しくてしかたがなかった学会活動も、どこか先が見えない、空気が抜けたような気がしていました。この一年間、主婦同盟の活動も、私たちの活動を本当に理解してくださる池田先生に伝わっているのかどうか、不安になってきました。私たちもなにか芯（しん）が定まっていないような、大事なことを避けているように思えてきました。

池田先生の行動を私たちが知るようになったのは、第五次の中国訪問を終えた昭和五十五年四月二十九日、長崎空港に戻られて以降のことでした。翌日五月一日、池田先生

101

は九州の青年を激励され、五月三日には関西文化会館での「創価学会の日」記念勤行会、四日に大阪支部長会、五日は「後継者の日」記念勤行会で小学生・中学生・高校生たちを激励し、男子部部長会、女子部部長会、関西同志の集いに出席されております。

池田先生が私たちの会合に出席されるようになりました。新たな戦いが開始されたことを知りました。一年前の異様な総会の後、池田先生は神奈川文化会館で、「正義」の二文字、そして「共戦」を揮毫され、たった一人、戦いをすすめられていたことをのちに知りました。

池田先生が私たちのもとに帰ってきてくださった。その喜びを胸に、池田先生との共戦を誓って、私たち広島主婦同盟も挑戦を開始しました。広島で活動する私たちの、一番の使命を果たそうと誓いました。主婦同盟の広島での活動として、被爆体験をみなさんにうかがって、生の声をテープに収めよう、証言を文集として遺そうとしました。まず、町ごとに二十名ほどの人に、原爆にあった人に、平和のためにぜひ、その時の模様を語ってくださいと、最初は全部で百四十人の方にお願いしました。みなさんに断られました。

うちにはいままだ娘がおります、息子がおります、親が被爆者ということが分かったら、縁談がみな壊れてしまうので、いっさい知られたくない。──なにか、まるで伝染病をもっているように、思われていたのです。

102

終戦から三十五年後、原爆の被害は被爆二世にまで拡大され膨れ上がっていました。親が放射能を浴びているので、その子どもが結婚して授かった赤ちゃんも障害児が生まれていると、事実以外にもいろいろな風評が流れておりました。みなさんに敬遠されました。何回、お願いしても、一人もこころよい返事はくれませんでした。

記録に残されて、本などにされて公表されては困りますといわれました。

お気持ちはよく理解できました。私も長男を原爆症で亡くし、のちに授かった二人の子どものことを日々心配しつづける歳月を過してきましたので、身に染みて感じとれます。どうしか証言を遺すことが、私たちの、世界の人々にたいする使命なのだと思いました。どうかお話を聞かせてくださいと、訴えてつづけて三年間、三百名を超える方々に、辛抱強くお願いして、やっと、百余名の方の了解が得られました。自宅におうかがいし、体験を語ってもらい、テープに録ることがはじまりました。あらたまった堅苦しいことでは、お気持ちも表われませんので、一人ひとりに「広島弁そのままで、そのときのことを話してください」とお願いしました。

住所は載せないでください、約束してください、と多くの方が望まれました。生年や被爆された場所は正確なものですが、約束したとおり、後にどこに移り住んだかは伏せまし

103

た。運動をはじめてから五年かかり、ようやく昭和六十年五月に本にまとめることができました。私も、被爆者の一人として証言を載せていただきました。文集は、広島県の小学校・中学校の全校、県庁、市役所、図書館、平和資料館に贈らせていただきました。その文集『語り継ごう　業火の中のさけび』の「まえがき」に広島主婦同盟議長として、私は次のように、書かせていただきました。

「被爆四十年、広島の街々には緑の木々が生い繁り、最先端の服装を身につけ、行き交う輝くような顔の若人からは、とてもあの時の悲惨さは、想像だにできず、人々の頭の中には次第に、あの時のことが時の流れの中で風化しかけているのではないでしょうか？　と、広島を訪れた友人に言われた時、私は即座に友の言葉を、さえぎったものでした。

いくら街が新しく、きれいになり、足の伸びやかな若人が、軽やかに市内を歩き回ろうと、あの時の、あの一瞬を目にし、肉親を亡くした者にとって、生命ある限りあの時のことは、忘れ去ることはできません。

私達、広島主婦同盟は〝子供らに残せる社会を作ろう〟とのテーマに基き、被爆者の生の声をテープに収め、それを文集として残す作業を、昭和五十五年より行ってまいりました。

104

しだいにうすれゆく記憶と、あの時の悲惨さは二度と思い出したくないと、固く口を閉ざされる被爆者の方々に幾度となく、お会いしてきました。収録の約束をし、数日後行ってみますと、「ガンで入院しました」と、家族の方の悲しい顔。そして亡くなられたとの報に接した時、〝もっと早くお会いしとけば良かった〞の思いにかられたものでした。私も十七歳で被爆し、原爆病で生後間もない長男を亡くした悲しみを持っているだけに人ごととは思えないつらさでした。こうした悲しみをのりこえて何とか百余名の方の声を文集としてまとめることができました。この文集は、被爆場所をエリア別に大別して編集いたしました。

とつとつと語られる広島弁を、そのまま文集として書き留めましたので、読みにくい部分もあろうかと思います。又紙面の都合上、内容の一部を割愛させて頂きましたので、御了承下さいませ。

広島主婦同盟全員、この文集を作成することにより、一歩でも二歩でも世界平和への礎を築くために貢献できればとの祈りをこめて作業にあたりました。

最後に出版にあたり、快く収録に御協力して下さった皆様に心より御礼申し上げます。」

併せて、編集に携わった方々の当時のご苦労を思い起し、深い深い感謝の意を込めて、

お名前をここに記させていただきます。

「天部恵子　井上美恵子　上野和子　片山睦子　北村良子　桐原澄子　小出桂子　桜井恭子　下地博子　新沢末子　新谷澄江　千手ミツエ　竹岡智佐子　武田定子　辰己美弥子　田崎邦子　長岡啓子　西岡恵美子　橋口鈴子　浜縁れい子　平岡操　深井正子　古川公子　増田正子　松浦悦子　松崎貞枝　宮川久子　村上明子　山川冨美子　山中エミ子」

収録をはじめてから、文集を発刊するまでのあいだに、二人の方がガンで、すでに亡くなっていました。あれからさらに二十年余の歳月が過ぎました。百余名の方のうち半数以上を占める、明治・大正のお生まれの方の多くが、この間に亡くなっています。若い部類に属している私も、すでに八十歳代になっています。昭和五十五年、池田先生の新たな戦いに呼応しようと、心を定めてはじめた被爆体験の収録は、このころがほぼ最後のチャンスだったのだと、振り返って思います。

日本にいる私たちと同じように、海外の多くの会員の方が池田先生の指導を求めておられたのだと思います。昭和五十六年（一九八一年）になると、池田先生は一月からアメリカ指導に旅立たれました。その多忙ななか、五月には四日間にもわたり、5・3「創価学

106

会の日）記念勤行会・祝賀の集いが、創価大学中央体育館・グラウンドで行われました。私たちも招待され、五月三日の勤行会・祝賀の集いに参加することができました。

勤行会が終わり、体育館の後ろから大学の講義棟につづく渡り廊下の近くで誠治を待っているとき、池田先生がそこを通りかかりました。失礼にならないように控えなければいけない、どうしようと思っていても体は先生の方に向かってしまいます。行動の早い先生は見る間に私たちに近づき「竹岡さんのお母さんですね。よくこられました。ゆっくり東京を楽しんでから、広島に戻られてください」と声をかけてくださいました。こんな大変なときにも、私たちのことを気遣ってくださるのかと胸が熱くなりました。握手をしてくださいました。差し出された手をそっと両手で握りながら、私はなにもいえず、おもわず、

「先生！　お元気で頑張ってください！」と声を出していました。それしか、言葉がなかったのです。

広島に帰ってから二日後、東京の誠治から電話がかかってきました。

「先生と握手していただいたとき、お母さん、なにかいった？」

「もうとっさのことで、言葉もなんも出てこんから、お元気で頑張ってください、としか

107

いえんかったよ。あとで考えてみたら、頑張ってくださいなんて失礼なことを、と思う

て、夜も寝れんかったんよ」

「そうか。先生はよろこんでおられたよ。竹岡君のお母さんに励まされましたと、婦人部

から激励されて、大変によろこんでおられたよ。『池田先生が頑張ってくださらなければ、

創価学会は潰れてしまいますから、お願いします！ ということを母は伝えたかったので

す』とお話ししたよ」

　私は顔から火が出るくらい、恥ずかしくなりました。同時に池田先生の温かいお気持ち

が伝わってきました。ああっ、先生はこんなにまでして心をくだいてくださっている。きっ

と、私が悩んでいると思われて、息子に伝えたのだと思います。

　数日後、池田先生が海外指導に旅立たれたことを知りました。ソ連、西ドイツ、ブルガ

リア、オーストリア、イタリア、フランス、アメリカと、北半球を一周する六十一日にも

およぶ歴訪でした。出発前の激務のなかで、私たちのことを気遣い誠治に声をかけたこと

を知り、また感謝の思いが、熱く、熱く込み上げてきました。私は、私の使命をはたそう

と、あらためて決意を固めました。

被爆体験文集の編纂作業が軌道にのりはじめた時、ついに私の願いが実現しました。昭和五十七年（一九八二年）、ニューヨークで開催される第二回国連軍縮特別総会に行くことになりました。すでに国連の活動を支援するNGO（非政府組織）団体になっていた創価学会が、総会に代表団を派遣するにあたり、広島・長崎から被爆者の代表も参加することになったのです。私はその一員になりました。

三十七年前、あの冷たくなった赤ちゃんの体を抱いた時、アメリカに行って、この惨状を直接伝えようと心に決めてから、ずっと願い、祈りつづけていたことです。広島に原爆を投下したエノラ・ゲイ機の副機長だったロバート・ルイス大尉は、投下直後のきのこ雲を見て「おお神よ、われわれは何ということをしてしまったのだ」とメモに書きつけたことを明かしています。アメリカで一九五五年（昭和三十年）にテレビで放映されたドキュメンタリー番組のことです。しかし、そのきのこ雲の下で、ルイス大尉が想像さえできないほど悲惨なできごとがつづいていたことを、私は知っています！　それを語りにニューヨークにきたのです。

国連軍縮特別総会は、六月七日に開幕しました。その四日前の六月三日には、国連本部で「現代世界の核の脅威」展が行われています。広島・長崎の青年たちが企画したもので

す。六日に池田先生の「軍縮提言」が国連代表部でキタニ総会議長に手渡されました。総会にあわせて行われた反核集会は、十二日のセントラル・パークでの百万人集会が焦点となりました。

数日前に行った私たち被爆者の証言は、テレビ、ラジオを通じて三十回を超えてアメリカ全土に伝えられ、ニューヨークタイムスをはじめとする各紙が報道しました。

その夜、会場となったルーズベルトホテルの広間に、たくさんのアメリカの人が集まってくださいました。私は被爆の体験をできるだけ感情を抑えて語りました。母を捜し回った私が見た惨状、亡くなった長男のこと、二人の子どもたちにも放射線の影響があるのではないかという不安。込み上げる気持ちを、抑えに抑えて語りました。とうとう抑えきれなくなって、最後に私は何回も訴えました。

「アメリカのみなさん。私は、命を懸けて！ このニューヨークにやってきました！ どうか、こんな恐ろしい爆弾を二度と再び作らないで、また使わないでください。世界の平和と核兵器の廃絶をどうかお願いします。私たちが味わった、人間としてこんな惨めなことを、二度とだれにも味わわせてはなりません！」

証言を終えた後、会場のいちばん後ろから大きな男の人が立ち上がって、私の方に歩いてきました。私の席の傍らに立ったまま、最初はなにもいいません。しばらくして、ぽろ

110

ぽろと涙を流し、私の手をとりました。「タケオカさん。私は、悪いことをしました。広島に帰られたら、今日の話を大勢の人に伝えて、いつまでも頑張ってください」といいます。私はその方の手をぎゅーと握りしめました。この人の胸のなかに平和の灯火が、強い、私の願いが、一つ灯ったのだ。これが、私の使命だったのだ。この灯火が全アメリカに、全世界に広がっていけ、と祈って握りしめました。

同時に、すうっと頭によぎるものがありました。この人の最初の言葉です。「私は、悪いことをしました」といいました。どういう意味だろう？「アメリカは」といったら大変なことになるから「私は」といったのだろうか？　通訳さんにお願いして、五分間ほどその方と話をすることができました。ジョン・モンゴメリーというお名前で、ハーバード大学の行政学部長をなさっている方でした。

被爆体験を語る集会が終了した後に、モンゴメリーさん、ノーベル生理学・医学賞を受賞したハーバード大学教授ジョージ・ウォールドさん、マンハッタン計画に参画した物理学者でマサチューセッツ工科大学教授バーナード・フェルトさんの三人と、私たち被爆者との対話会が開かれました。科学的データや数値では分からない、被爆の実状を私たちの話からつかみ取ろうと、みな熱心に耳を傾けてくださいました。直接、被爆者と語り合う

111

ことは、三人にとって、どんなにか複雑な心境だったかと思われます。三人とも言葉は少なかったのですが、いちばん寡黙だったフェルトさんが最後に「時代がどう変わっても、核の悲劇を二度とくり返してはいけない。あらゆる手段を使って、核兵器による全滅の危機を回避していかなければならない」と語ってくださいました。

モンゴメリーさんはその後、何度も広島の平和公園を訪れ、資料館の三百人入るホールで講演をされました。そして、広島の復興に尽くされ、平和のための活動をつづけられました。広島の復興に全力を傾注されたモンゴメリー博士夫妻を記念して、広島池田平和記念館で「モンゴメリー桜」の植樹が行われたのは、平成三年（一九九一年）のことでした。

モンゴメリーさんの講演を、私はいつもいちばん前の席で聞かせていただきました。それまで二度、私は迷惑になってはいけないと遠慮しておりましたが、三度目の平成十一年（一九九九年）十一月、講演が終了してから追いかけて行き、「しばらくですね」と挨拶をしました。そのときモンゴメリーさんは、日本語で「あっ、タケオカさん。生きていた！ああ、よかった。生きていた！」と、私を抱きかかえて喜んでくださいました。ニューヨークで会ってからずっと、私のことを気にかけてくれていたのです。思い切って挨拶をしてよかったと思いました。

112

モンゴメリーさんは行政学者で、都市計画の専門家でしたが、昭和十七年（一九四二年）から二十一年（一九四六年）の四年間、軍人として服役しておりました。原爆投下から半年後、占領軍政府の一員として広島に赴任した二十六歳のモンゴメリーさんは、広島市復興局の再建計画委員会の顧問となり、廃墟となった市内をつぶさに調査していたのです。

本当にやさしい方なのです。戦争になれば、軍人として命令には従わなければなりません。戦争どんなにやさしい生命の方も、鬼の命に変えてしまう戦争こそ私たちの敵なのです。

を容認し、アメリカ軍の一員として、結果として核の開発に参加してしまった自分の責任を強く感じていたのでした。

ニューヨークでお会いした時に「私は、悪いことをしました」といったのは、モンゴメリーさんの誠実さの証でした。モンゴメリーさんは著書『ヒロシマ・ベトナム・核』の「日本語版への序文」のなかに「私が、本書の結論で述べるような考えをもつにいたったのは、創価学会インターナショナルが主催した国連での核凍結の討論会に出席したからである」と書いておられます。その一年半後の昭和五十九年（一九八四年）一月、モンゴメリーさんは池田先生と渋谷の国際友好会館でお会いになっております。池田先生の一九九一年九月二十六日のハーバード大学での講演で、名誉教授になられたモンゴメリーさんは池田先

生の略歴と功績を紹介するプレゼンテイターを務められました。

　被爆体験を語るために、私がロシアに行ったのは平成十三年（二〇〇一年）九月のことです。広島平和文化センターの館長さんから依頼があり、ボルゴグラード（旧スターリングラード）市を訪れました。広島市とは昭和四十七年（一九七二年）九月に姉妹都市提携をしております。広島市と長崎市は共同で、平成七年（一九九五年）から核保有国の都市を中心に、「ヒロシマ・ナガサキ原爆展」を開催しております。ボルゴグラードでは九月八日から十月七日までの開催でした。

　今回は、同行してくれた夫といっしょの平和行動です。九月五日、成田空港を飛び立ち、ほぼ十時間でモスクワに到着しました。ひんやりとした風のなか、紅葉した樹々がうつくしく揺れています。翌日、長崎から被爆体験を語るために到着した男性の方、センターの館長さん私たちの四人は、飛行機でボルゴグラード市に移動しました。副市長さん、国立スターリングラード攻防戦パノラマ博物館副館長、通訳の方たちに迎えられ、私たちの平和行動がはじまりました。

　原爆展の会場となった博物館の二階には、第二次大戦中のドイツ軍とのすさまじい攻防

114

戦を描いた、巨大なパノラマがあります。スターリングラードの攻防戦では、一九四二年六月から四三年二月まで、人類史上最大の市街戦が九か月もつづけられたのです。ソ連軍四十八万人、民間人四万人、ドイツ軍側（ドイツ、ハンガリー、ルーマニア、イタリア）も四十万人にものぼる死者が出ています。この攻防戦だけで、死傷者あわせて百五十万人もの方の人生が狂わされ台なしにされたのです。なんと悲惨なことか、戦争とはなんと残酷なことか、私はあらためて思い知らされました。

ボルゴグラード市訪問にあたり、著書『私のソビエト紀行』をはじめとする池田先生のソビエト、ロシアにかんする指導を、私は何度も読み返しました。池田先生は、昭和四十九年（一九七四年）九月八日、初のソ連訪問の旅に出発されました。創価学会第二代会長の戸田城聖先生が「原水爆禁止宣言」を発表された日と、同じ日です。戸田先生は昭和三十二年（一九五七年）九月八日、横浜の三ツ沢競技場で行われた体育大会の席上、五万人の青年に向かって、原子爆弾を使用する者は魔ものであると宣言し、この思想を全世界に広めることが日本の若人の使命であると、遺訓しました。

広島に生まれ育ち、そして被爆した私の、宿命を使命にかえる原点となる遺訓です。あらためて一字一句を生命に刻みこむために、ここに全文を写させていただきます。

「天竜も諸君らの熱誠にこたえてか、きのうまでの嵐はあとかたもなく、天気晴朗のこの日を迎え、学会魂を思うぞんぶんに発揮せられた諸君ら、またそれにこたえるこの大観衆の心を、心から喜ばしく思うものであります。

さて、きょうの喜ばしさにひきかえて、今後とも難があるかも知らん。あるいは身にいかなる攻撃を受けようかと思うが、諸君らに今後、遺訓すべき第一のものを、本日は発表いたします。

まえまえから申しているように、次の時代は青年によって担われるのである。広宣流布は、われわれの使命であることは申すまでもないことであり、これはぜひともやらんければならんことであるが、今、世に騒がれている核実験、原水爆実験にたいする私の態度を、本日、はっきりと声明したいと思うものであります。いやしくも私の弟子であるならば、私のきょうの声明を継いで、全世界にこの意味を浸透させてもらいたいと思うのであります。

それは、核あるいは原子爆弾の実験禁止運動が、今、世界に起こっているが、私はその奥に隠されているところの爪をもぎ取りたいと思う。それは、もし原水爆を、いずこの国であろうと、それが勝っても負けても、それを使用したものは、ことごとく死刑にすべき

であるということを主張するものであります。

なぜかならば、われわれ世界の民衆は、生存の権利をもっております。その権利をおび

やかすものは、これ魔ものであり、サタンであり、怪物であります。それを、この人間社会、

たとえ一国が原子爆弾を使って勝ったとしても、それを使用したものは、こと

ごとく死刑にされねばならんということを、私は主張するものであります。

たとえ、ある国が原子爆弾を用いて世界を征服しようとも、その民族、それを使用した

ものは悪魔であり、魔ものであるという思想を全世界に広めることこそ、全日本青年男女

の使命であると信ずるものであります。

願わくは、きょうの体育大会における意気をもって、この私の第一回の声明を全世界に

広めてもらいたいことを切望して、きょうの訓示にかえるしだいであります。」

戸田先生のこの宣言の重要性は、当時すでに信心をはじめていた母が私に伝えてくれま

した。母は孫たちにも教えていました。私がロシアの学生さんたちに体験を語る日も、ちょ

うど九月八日ごろになることをうかがいました。私は必死になり、真剣に池田先生の指導

を読んでロシア訪問を迎える日々をすごしました。

ニューヨークのときと同じように、今回も私にとっては、核兵器の使用は「絶対悪」だ

と強く主張する池田先生とともに行う、平和のための戦いだったのです。ボルゴグラードでは国立大学の二校で被爆の体験を語らせていただきました。私の孫と同世代になる学生さんたちは、英知に輝く真剣な眼差しで、身じろぎもせずに聞き入ってくれました。講演終了後、学長さんも加わり学生さんたちとの記念撮影が行われました。

撮影が終わると、学生さんが何人も私を囲んで、口々にいいます。「自分たちの国、ロシアにもまだ大量の核兵器がある。今日の話しを聞いて、二度と原子爆弾を使わせてはならない、絶対に使わせてはならないと決めました。私たちも平和への活動をはじめますので、どうか、広島に帰られても、お体を大切にして頑張ってください」と激励してくださいました。私は、この学生さんたち、私の孫の世代、さらに若い人たちに語り継いでいくことの大切さを、痛切に感じました。

私が広島市の「広島平和記念資料館被爆体験証言者」（語り部）の一人として、体験をみなさんに語るようになったのは、平成元年（一九八九年）からです。今日まで二十年を超えてつづけてきたことになります。はじめは、市での少人数の会議からはじまりました。証言者を募ることも課題でした。現在全国から広島にきていただかなければなりません。

のように軌道にのるには数年かかっております。

中学校、高等学校の生徒さんたちに語ることが多いので、五月と十一月など修学旅行の
シーズンには、一日に二会場で証言する日々がつづきます。大阪の市役所の職員の方、家
族の方が広島にこられるのは、すでに二十回を超えています。広島市内の小学校では、毎
年私の体験を聞いてもらっております。この二十年で千回をとうに超え、私の証言を聞い
てくださった方は五万人以上になっています。

被爆証言の活動をなさる方の人数は当初も、現在も同じ三十人ほどですが、この二十年
の間に亡くなられた方、ご高齢で辞められた方も増えてきました。あらたに加わってくだ
さる方のおかげで人数が保たれているのです。証言者の方は、みなさん後遺症を抱えてい
るのですから、交替していかなければなりません。こうしたなか、二十年間つづけること
ができたのは、私が持った信仰のなかで教えられた、平和のための強い使命感の故です。

私も夏になると具合が悪くなります。七月、八月になると熱があるわけでもないのに、
体がだるくなり掌が暑くなります。お医者さんに診てもらっても、ほかにはどこにも異常
がみられません。甲状腺からくるのだといわれています。自分だけかと思って被爆された
みなさんに聞くと、やはり私と同じ症状が出ています。これは六十五年間ずっと同じです。

しかし、証言を希望されたときは、断ることはなりません。それは私の使命なのですから、少々頭痛がし、つらいときでも、とんぷくを飲んで、話をするためにでかけます。

誠治の息子、光城が中学二年生になったとき、夏休みに一人で広島にくることになりました。私は、この機会に市内を案内しながら孫に、戦争の話、母と私が被爆したときのことを伝えることにしました。五年かかって、ようやく文集を発刊した年のことです。八月に入り、またいつものように掌が暑くなってきていました。

数日かけて、中央公園にある広島城、縮景園、原爆ドーム、平和記念公園を巡りながら、話をすすめていきました。亡くなった長男のこと、アメリカで核兵器を開発した科学者と話をしたこと、すべてを伝えようと急がずにゆっくりと語っていきました。熱心に耳を傾け、真剣に聞いてくる光城の姿に、私は確信しました。私たちの平和への願いは、この子たちに伝えることができる。あらためて、未来に生きる子どもたちのために、この道を進もうと決めました。

原爆慰霊碑の前では、池田先生が十年前、此処で献花をされ、唱題されたことを光城に伝えました。私は光城に、これから世界中の指導者が広島にきて、この場所で祈りを捧げ

るようになるためにお題目をあげようといいました。

昭和五十年（一九七五年）十一月、池田先生は原爆慰霊碑に献花された翌日、広島県立体育館で行われた一万人が参加した第三十八回本部総会での一時間にわたる大講演で私たちを激励してくださいました。冒頭池田先生は「今回の本部総会が、原爆投下の地、広島県下で開かれましたことは、戦後三十年という一つの節を迎えて、二度と再びあの人類の惨劇を繰り返してはならないという、私どもの重大なる決意をもって行われていることを、まずははっきりと申し上げておきたい」と述べられました。一万人の参加者の一人として先生の「私どもの重大なる決意」という言葉に胸が燃え上がりました。

次に池田先生は「健康・青春の本質」についてふれられ、「健康とは、ただたんに病気ではない、という状態をさすものではありません。……どのような苦難をも乗り越え、最悪の環境条件さえも、かえって飛躍の原動力に変えていくところに、真実の健康像がある」と教えてくださいました。さらに「一人の生命の心身両面にわたる健康と青春の息吹は、たんなる一個の人間革命にとどまらず、大きくは病める社会、国土の蘇生にもつながっていくことを確信」してくださいと、広島の私たちに激励してくださいました。私たち自身が真に健康になることが、この原爆におかされた広島の国土の蘇生をもたらすのだと教え

てください。

さらに「朝鮮戦争において、中東紛争において、さらにベトナム戦争においても、何回となく核戦争の瀬戸際に立たされましたが、かろうじて人類が核を使う誘惑をしりぞけることができたのも、まさしく広島の地よりわき起こった平和への熱願によるものといえましょう。その意味で広島は、世界の核戦争を防止する平和の原点であり聖地である、……核兵器の恐ろしさをもっともよく知っているのは日本人であり、私ども日本人こそ、それを全世界に訴える資格と責任をもっている」と、私たちの使命の重大さを教えてください。

ました。私は、私の宿命を使命にかえて、その使命の道を歩もうと決めました。

中学生の孫に被爆体験を伝えることができた喜びを、私は手紙に託して池田先生に報告させていただきました。すると思いもかけず、池田先生は私と光城の話をモデルの一つにされて、『ヒロシマへの旅』という小説に書いてくださり、中学生文化新聞に昭和六十一年（一九八六年）八月から翌六十二年二月まで連載されました。中学二年生の「一城」君に広島を案内し被爆体験を伝える「八重子おばさん」という設定で、私の体験も内容に入れていただきました。いつも、いつも池田先生は私たちに応えてくれます、激励してくださいます。

原爆慰霊碑の前で二人で唱題をしているとき、私は、私たちを支えてきた信心の凄さに思いを馳せていました。絶望していた人生がたしかに変わりました、生きることの素晴らしさを知ることができました。その信心の道を、母リョウと私たち夫婦、二人の子ども誠治と真里子、そして伸子、光城、絵美、正幸たち孫の世代と、四代に亘って歩んできました。そのときから、さらに二十年の時が経過しました。私たち一家の信心の功徳は次の五代へと流れていきます。今年平成二十二年（二〇一〇年）三月、私たちにひ孫、香織が誕生したのです。

四代、五代に亘る私の家族の信心の功徳を支えてくださったのは、いつも、いつも私たちを激励してくださる、池田先生と奥様でした。母リョウは、池田先生が第三代会長に就任されたことを報ずる聖教新聞を掲げて「これで世界が変わる！　救われる」と断言していました。私たち夫婦はあの地獄の底に閉じ込められたような生活から、学会活動をとおして救われました。人生の喜びと使命を知りました。そして節目ごとに幾度も直接あたたかい激励をいただきました。私たちは池田先生と奥様の励ましによって、使命の道を歩むことができたのです。池田先生・奥様、本当に、本当に、ありがとうございます。感謝の気持ちは書ききれません。

私は故あって広島に生まれ、原爆に遭ったのだと知りました。多くの方が語りたがらなかった、その悲惨さ、残酷さを若い人たちに伝える道を私は選びました。原爆の悲惨さ、残酷さは私たちでしか語れないことなのですから。日本を「最初の」被爆国にしてはなりません。日本は「唯一の」被爆国にしなければいけません。あの惨状を、どの国のだれにたいしてもくり返させてはなりません。二度と核兵器を、どこにおいても使用させてはなりません。この思いを孫たちや孫、さらにその子どもたちに伝えるという大きな使命が、池田先生が教えてくださった私の使命が、私を生きさせてきたのです。

124

『ヒロシマの宿命を使命にかえて』の発刊に寄せて

竹岡誠治

私は小学校に上がるまで丸坊主で、頭に髪の毛が一本もなかった。他の子どもには黒い髪がいっぱい生えているのに、自分だけツルツルなのはどうしてだろうと思っていた。また、私は妹の真里子と二人兄妹で、自分は長男だとずっと思っていたが、じつは次男だった。

この二つのことのわけが判明したのは、祖母によってだった。「おまえはピカドンのせいで頭に髪が生えないんだよ」「おまえには、じつは兄がいて生後ほどなくして亡くなったのよ。真っ黒になって、かわいそうでならなかったよ」と祖母から伝えられたのは、いつだったか。そのとき初めて「ピカドン」という言葉を聞き、それが「原子爆弾」というアメリカが日本に落とした新型爆弾だと知ったときの驚愕は、今でも鮮明に覚えている。

私の祖母・國貞リョウ(一九〇三〜一九六七)は陸軍病院の看護婦長だった。昭和二十年八月六日午前八時十五分、米軍爆撃機エノラ・ゲイが広島に原爆を投下した時、祖母は何日も病院に泊まり込んで任務にあたっており、爆心地から少し南の舟入で被爆した。爆風で片目を失い、身

体の約二〇〇か所にガラスの破片が刺さった。命だけはとり止め、一週間もうろうと、被爆者が収容されていた学校の教室で生死の境を行き来していた。

母・智佐子はその時十七歳。女子挺身隊の奉仕中で、たまたま友人と宮島に行く予定で、己斐上町（爆心地より西に約三キロメートル）の家から出かける寸前に被爆し、後ろの畑まで吹き飛ばされ意識を失った。しばらくして意識が戻り、母親を探して爆心地をさまよい歩いた。その時、十七歳の乙女が目の当たりにした惨状は、筆舌に尽くしがたかったものに違いない。

直接には原爆による損傷を受けていなかったものの、直後の一週間、広島市内を歩き回ったことで、母の身体は肺から、皮膚から、血脈の深部まで、後々まで強いダメージとなる影響を受けていた。いわゆる「間接被爆」であった。一週間の後、奇跡的に祖母を見つけ出した母は、大八車に祖母を乗せて自宅に連れ帰り、寝たきりの被爆病人を献身的に介護した。

敗戦後の混乱の時代に、縁あって結婚、出産。希望を見いだしかけた人生が再び挫折したのは、急に黒い斑点が出て、体が真っ黒となり、とても人間の子とは思われない。それでも懸命に子育てに取り組んだ母の、その子が落命したときの、哀しさ、辛さは想像に余りあるものがある。寝たきりで治療を続ける母親を抱え、結婚生活が軌道に乗り始めた矢先の長男の死である。

こうした不孝の連続のなかで、いつしか夫は酒に溺れるようになり、時には暴力を振るうようになる。

昭和二十三年十二月十四日、次男が誕生。名前は誠治。私は小さいころ「セイボークン」

生まれ出でた最愛の男の子に「原爆症」が表われたからだ。

と呼ばれていた。「誠坊君」である。

私は祖母に育てられた。寝るときは両親は一階、私はやっと歩けるようになった祖母と一緒に二階に寝ていた。もの心がついたころは、家の中は夫婦喧嘩の連続で、病身の祖母はいつの間にか二階の部屋に仏壇を安置し「南無妙法蓮華経」と題目をあげるようになっていた。聞いてみると、日蓮正宗創価学会（のちに日蓮正宗から独立した創価学会）に入会したという。昭和二十九年のことである。

私は日蓮宗というのは身延と聞いていたから、ウチのオバアチャンは変な新興宗教に入信してしまったのだと思っていた。そのうちに、わが家の二階は座談会場となって、夜になるとミニ集会が行われるようになった。集会にみえる人々は、みんな貧乏で、病人で、悲惨な人が多かった。

でも、いい人たちばかりだった。

ある夜、玄関先でバタッ！　と大きな音がした。覗いてみると中年の男の人が倒れている。「どうしたんねー」と聞くと、バス代がなくて座談会場のウチまで遠くから歩いてきた。おナカがすいて、倒れてしまったという。オバアチャンが「チイチャン（母のこと）、おにぎりつくって食べさせてあげんさい」。すると父が「ウチはどこの馬の骨か分からん奴に喰わせるメシはない！」と怒鳴りだし、一階のステレオのボリュームをいっぱいに上げて、座談会の妨害を始める。そんな日々が続いていた。

私はオバアチャンを助けようと思い、邪宗教に入信するつもりで「オバアチャン、ワシが入信

127

したら幸福か」と聞いた。「そりゃー、セイボークンが入信してくれたら、こんなうれしいことはない」。こうして私は「南無妙法蓮華経」と題目を唱えはじめた。その後、父と母も信心をはじめることとなり、昭和三十四年十一月七日に創価学会に入会した。私は昭和三十五年三月五日、春休みを利用して富士の大石寺に参詣登山しようということになり、その際に御授戒を受け正式に創価学会の会員となった。

ある日、オバアチャンが片目しかない眼からポロポロと涙を流し、新聞を揺らしながら「ガォー、ガォー」と叫んでいた。ついに気がふれたのかと思った私は「オバアチャン、どうしたんねん」と聞くと、「これで大丈夫！ これでええんじゃ、これでええんじゃ」と喜び勇んでいるではないか。ゆっくりと聞きほどくと、それは、池田大作先生が創価学会の第三代会長に就任したことを報じた聖教新聞の記事のためであった。

当時は、昭和三十三年四月に第二代会長戸田城聖先生が亡くなり、これで創価学会も空中分解するだろうと、マスコミが書き立てていた時代である。オバアチャンも多くの人々にこの信心を勧めていたこともあり、どうなるのかと不安を抱いていた最中であった。

「池田先生が会長に就任してくれた。もうこれで創価学会は誰からも後ろ指さされんどー。これで創価学会は大丈夫なんじゃ」と歓喜の涙を流していたのであった。

「そんなにこの池田先生というのはえらいんか」と私は聞いた。

「おおそうじゃ。ひと目でええけえ、生きているうちに池田先生に会いたいもんじゃ」

128

それを聞いた瞬間、私は池田先生という人にこの人生をかけてみようと思った。原爆によって

これ以上はないという悲惨を味わわされた竹岡家が、創価学会の信心によって希望の灯を点され

ていたのは子供心にもよく分かっていたからだった。その時から、朝晩に法華経の方便品と寿量

品の読誦をはじめた。いわゆる勤行である。

その後、父・清、母・智佐子は、支部長、婦人部長という役職もいただき、東に西に、学会活

動に日々奔走をはじめた。私も高等部（現未来部のうちの高校生の組織）に所属して活動をはじ

めた。

昭和四十一年の暮れ、私の通う私立修道高等学校の畠眞實先生から「おい竹岡！ お前に手紙

が届いているぞ」と言われ、一通の封書を受け取った。封書には「修道高校三年竹岡誠治様」と

宛名があり、差出人には「宮本孝史」とあった。私には、まったく心当たりがなかった。わけの

分からないまま封をきると、そこには「文集を読んで君に手紙を出した。大学進学にあたっては、

是非とも東京の大学を受けよ。その時には下記に連絡せよ。学生部第十四部部長宮本孝史」（趣意）

とあった。

私の家は父は中国電力の社員で、ごく普通のサラリーマン（後に電産組合の委員長までやるが）。

父母からは「大学に行くんなら、国立だけよ。広島大学に行きんしゃい。それならええけんね。

国立ならええよ」と常々言われていたので、仕送りが発生する東京の大学に行こうとは、これぽっ

ちも考えていなかった。

祖母から「池田先生にひと目会いたい、ひと目会いたい」と聞いていた私は、手紙を受け取ってからムラムラと、東京に行ってもいいか、との思いが頭をもたげてきた。しかし、苦労して育ててもらった両親にわがままも言えず、悩んでいた。

年が明けて、私は意を決して「私立は国立の前に受験があるけえ、予行演習のつもりで中央大学の法学部を受けたいけん、東京に行ってみたい」と父に頼んだ。父は「まあ、一回慣れてみるのもええけん、行ってこい」と応じた。

そこで、夜行寝台車で東京へ。東京駅に出迎えてくれたのは仲野皖一さんという学生部のグループ長であった。高田馬場にある仲野邸（お父上は公明党新宿区議会議員の仲野長寿氏）で初めて会った宮本孝史氏は「君が竹岡君か！　本陣東京（創価学会の本部が東京にある）に出てきて、われわれと一緒に学生部で広宣流布（創価学会の信心を布教して幸福な社会を築くこと）の活動をしようじゃないか」と握手を求めた。

「申し訳ありませんが、私は予行演習で中大に受験に来たんで、第一志望は広大法学部なんです。家は貧乏なので、とても東京には来れません」と応えた。

「でも竹岡君、東京に来たら、月に一回、池田先生に会わせてあげるよ」と宮本氏。

全身に電気が走った。えー、池田先生に会える！　しかも月に一回。私はその晩、真剣に仲野邸の仏壇に向い祈った。

「どうかご本尊様、中央大学法学部に合格させてください。そして東京で学生部として活動させ

てください。どうか池田先生に月一回会わせてください。そして人生の指針を与えてください！」

――これまで十八年間のすべてをぶつけて、真剣に祈った。

翌朝、仲野長寿氏の奥様から「これを持って試験に行きなさい」とおにぎりをいただいた。これまでの人生で、けっして忘れてはならない思いのつまったおにぎりであった。涙ながらいただいたおにぎりのおかげで、試験に全力を傾注することができた。

私は、合格への充分な手ごたえを確信して広島へ戻った。問題は父の説得である。私の大学受験の時期には体調をくずして入院していた祖母のところに、上京の報告に行った。もう、言葉もろくにしゃべれない祖母であったが「東京に行けば、池田先生に毎月会える」という私の言葉に、「行け――！」とひと言、鮮明に言葉を発した。「おやじが反対で」と私。「ワシの遺言じゃ！」と祖母。

そこに、中央大学法学部の合格通知が届いた。

祖母が霊山に旅立ったのは、昭和四十二年二月二十八日であった。

当時は、国立大学の試験の発表の前に私立の入学金と授業料を納めなければならなかった。父は「お金の余裕はないが、オバアチャンの遺言じゃあしようがないの。じゃが誠坊よ、東京に行くからには一所懸命勉強せいよ」と、入学金を払ってくれた。

いざ東京へ、出発の日。母は私に「誠治君、私はあなたを池田先生のところに兵隊としてさしあげると思って東京にやります。もう帰ってこんでええから、思う存分、池田先生の下で働いておいで」と告げた。目に涙をいっぱいにためながら、送り出してくれた。

131

「分かりました。行ってまいります」

私はその後、学生部で幹部となり、男子部では副男子部長、創価班（登山会や学会の活動での会合運営の整理にあたる、当時全国約五万人）全国委員長となった。山あり谷ありの人生であったが、さまざまな局面で何ら逡巡することなく、創価学会を護り、発展させる活動に従事できたのも、この母のひと言であったと心から感謝している。

今にして思えば私が十八歳の時、宮本氏の「月一回、池田先生に会わせてあげる」との言葉はウソではなかった。それは、毎月一回行われる本部幹部会（創価学会のメイン行事。今でも行われている）の整理担当役員に就くことであった。直接言葉を交わす訳ではないが、あるときは場内から、あるときは場外から、池田先生の勇姿を見れることは限りなき幸せであった。

その後、創価班全国委員長となり、一時期は毎日のように池田先生と会話することができる黄金の日々を味わった。これも、私が会っているのではなく、「行け―！」と言った祖母が、「兵隊にやったと思っています」と言った母が、池田先生にお会いしているのだという思いでお仕えしてきた。

今回、この母の手記を読んで、昭和四十二年春、母親を亡くし同時に希望を託した息子を手離さなければならなかった母の心境を、あらためて知った。海よりも深い両親の恩を感ぜざるをえない。

これまで「自分のことより創価学会のこと、自分の立場より池田先生の心情を」との思いで生

きてくることができた。おかげで多くの人々に守られてきた。もうだめだと、社会的死と、精神的死に直面しながらも、乗り越えることができた。財産などなにもないが、素晴らしい先輩や友人に恵まれている。

この場をかりて、父に感謝したい。今は脳梗塞を患って療養中で、かろうじて杖を使って歩ける状態であるが、幸いなことに頭はしっかりとしている。

「今の誠治があるのは、お父さんのおかげです。たくさんの友人に恵まれているのは、お父さん、あなたのおかげです。あなたはあらゆる人に差別なく、分け隔てなく、誰にたいしても親切にしてきた。困った人がいれば、世間体など気にしないで助けてあげてきた。私は、そのお父さんの姿を見て育ってきたのです。おかげで私もたくさんの人と友達になれました。ありがとう」

母にもきいてほしい。

「お母さん。お母さんのおかげで、私は先に行くべきか、避けるべきか、人生の岐路に立った時、迷わず、困難かもしれないが、自分を捨てて創価学会のために、会員のために、池田先生のために、これまで人生を全うする道を歩むことができました。お母さん、誠治は、これからもこの道を歩みます」

この母の手記は、原爆が惹き起こした、二度とこの地上に起こしてはならない悲惨を、後世に伝えるために、そして、その逃げようのない泥沼の地獄をさ迷っていた一家に、光を与えていただいた創価学会への、なかんずく池田大作先生への報恩感謝の思いから纏められました。

私からの最後のメッセージは、こうです。

「どんな人であれ、年齢や地位や身体や、出自に関係なく、確信をもってこのＳＧＩ（創価学会インタナショナル）の仏法を勧めてください。わが広島の竹岡家は、今にも死んでしまいそうな小柄な重度の原爆症に苦しんでいた祖母に、信心を勧めてくださった一人の方のおかげで救われたのです」

今年の三月十六日、孫が誕生した。池田先生の香峰子奥様の「香」の字をいただき香織と名づけられた。これで私の家族の信心は、五世代目となったのである。

祖母・國貞リョウ

両親・竹岡清、智佐子

本人・竹岡誠治、妻・茂子　妹・東野真里子、夫・東野幸二

長女・北林伸子、夫・北林大作　長男・竹岡光城

孫・北林香織

私が華であるとは言わないが、一人のリョウの入信によって、清、智佐子、誠治、茂子、伸子、光城、香織と五代にわたるロータスが花開いたのである。

どうか、私の後輩の皆様、目の前のどんな人にも、この信心を確信をもって勧めてください。

その人が、その次の世代が、あるいはさらにその次が、二千年前のハスの実が時が来たれば華を咲かせるように、必ずあなたの折伏弘教の努力は実るのです。

第二次世界大戦の一国をあげた国家神道による統制の下で、日蓮正宗さえも国家に迎合し、日蓮大聖人の精神を踏みにじり、神札を祀った。この大圧力のなかでも筋を曲げず、立正安国の精神を貫き通し、殉教した初代会長牧口常三郎先生。そして「この地球上から悲惨の二字をなくしたい」と戦後の荒野に一人立たれた戸田城聖第二代会長。さらに「一人の人間における偉大な人間革命は、やがて一国の宿命の転換をも成し遂げ、さらに全人類の宿命の転換をも可能にする」と断言された池田大作第三代会長。

「戦争ほど、悲惨なものはない」「戦争ほど、残酷なものはない。戦争のテーマのもと、

——この太陽と蓮華（サンロータス）を信じて。

二〇一〇年七月二十二日　ＪＡＬ機上にて

この本の上梓にあたり、三度も広島まで足を運んでくださった、私の第三文明社時代の友人五味時作氏と、デザインを担当してくれた、広島で小中高校と同級であった吉永聖児氏に、心より感謝申し上げます。

英語版発刊に寄せて

この母の本『ヒロシマの宿命を使命にかえて』は、もともと、これまでの私の生き様と後半生へ向かう思いを記して、還暦記念に出版した自著『サンロータスの旅人』（二〇一〇年十二月十四日発刊）にあわせて作製し、その出版パーティーに参加してくださった親しい友人たちに差し上げたものが、最初でありました。

その後、私の本と母・智佐子の本、二冊に対する反響は、格段に母のほうが大きく、母の本は、すでに三刷となっております。

このたび、多くの方より、是非、英文で出版したらどうか、との声をいただき、上梓するにいたりました。

この間の出来事を追記しますと、北林大作氏と私の長女である伸子夫妻の間に香織の弟、私にとって二人目の孫・正輝が、二〇一三年一月十五日に生まれました。

さらに、長男・光城が二〇一一年十二月に菊本加代子と結婚。二〇一三年の七月に、創価学

会男子部長およびSGI（創価学会インタナショナル）男子部長を拝命・就任。十月十日には、二人の間に私の三人目の孫となる男の子、正城が誕生しました。

この本には、母に加え、祖母・國貞リョウの体験も語られておりますが、祖母から見れば、私の孫は、五世代目の誕生となりました。これによって、わが一族は、原爆によって果てるはずであった宿命を転換し、信仰による蘇生と勝利の実証を示すことができたと思います。

私は、さらに拍車をかけて、報恩の誠をつくす覚悟で、一層、精進してまいります。

竹岡　誠治　二〇一四年七月三日　東京・愛宕にて

＊この本の英語版『Hiroshima：Forging a Mission from Misfortune Living as a Witness to the Atomic Bomb』は二〇一四年八月、スピークマン書店より発刊。

137

第三版の発行にあたって

　一瞬にして十数万人（推定）の尊い命をうばった原爆投下。その後、一週間も行方が分からなかった祖母・國貞リョウが、奇跡的に助けだされてから、七十三年の歳月がたちました。当時、十七歳だった母・智佐子は今年九十歳となりましたが、今なお現役で被爆体験を語りつづけています。

　そして、妹・真里子は、被爆体験の語り部の継承者として活動をつづけています。

　二〇一六年九月、光城が創価学会青年部長に就任。二〇一七年三月十日、光城と加代子に四人目の孫となる次男・勝城が誕生しました。死の淵から生還した祖母の命脈は、確実に太く強くづいています。

　なお、私が東京に出るきっかけをつくって頂いた宮本孝史さんが、本年六月八日に逝去されました。心から追悼申し上げ、感謝の意を表します。

　二〇一八年八月六日　東京・日本橋浜町にて

　　　　　　　　　　　　　　　　竹岡　誠治

138

「日本語版・英語版　合本」の発刊にあたって

このたび、二〇二三年五月十九日より二十一日まで、岸田文雄総理大臣によって「G7広島サミット」が開催されることになりました。世界のリーダーが、被爆地・広島に一堂に会することは、誠に意義深いものがあります。

本書の発刊は、二〇一〇年に日本語版の第一刷を発行してから十三年を経ております。この間に、父・清は二〇二〇年一月二日に、著者である母・智佐子は二〇二〇年十二月三十一日に永眠いたしました。

私の長男・光城は創価学会青年部長を卒業、職場は今年四月からSGI（創価学会インタナショナル）となり、世界の平和と繁栄に向け尽力しています。

私の妹が嫁いだ東野家では、幸華、蓮正、煌翔の三人の、母のひ孫が誕生し、竹岡家と合わせて七人となりました。

原爆の惨禍から辛うじて生還し、信心の命脈を創った祖母・国貞リョウから五代目にあたるのです。母・智佐子もさぞかし喜んでいることと思います。

二〇二三年四月十一日　沖縄恩納村にて

竹岡　誠治

139

著者略歴

竹岡智佐子（たけおか・ちさこ）

　1928年（昭和3年）2月、広島市内の八丁堀に生まれる。山中高等女学校を卒業。1945年（昭和20年）8月6日、爆心地より西約3kmの己斐上町の自宅前で被爆。「黒い雨」を浴びる。翌日から1週間、広島陸軍病院の看護婦長だった母親を探して広島市内を訪ね歩く。

　1959年（昭和34年）創価学会に入会。広島主婦同盟議長として15年間活動。被爆体験文集『語り継ごう　業火の中のさけび』を編纂。1982年（昭和57年）6月、ニューヨークで開催された第2回国連軍縮特別総会のときに、創価学会代表団の広島・長崎の被爆者代表として参加。マンハッタン計画に参画した物理学者も含む対話集会で、被爆体験を証言する。2001年（平成13年）9月、広島平和文化センターの依頼により、ロシアのボルゴグラード（旧スターリングラード）の国立大学2校で被爆体験を学生たちに語る。広島市の「広島平和記念資料館被爆体験証言者」（語り部）の一員として発足時より参加、以後20年を超える活動をつづける。

2020年（令和2年）12月31日永眠

本書の日本語版は
2010 年 11 月 初版
2015 年 4 月 2 版
2018 年 8 月 3 版

英語版は
2014 年 8 月

いずれもスピークマン書店より発刊されました

日本語版・英語版 合本

ヒロシマの宿命を使命にかえて
——原爆の語り部として生きる

2023 年 5 月 3 日 初版 1 刷発行

著 者 竹岡智佐子

発行者 竹岡誠治

発行所 一般社団法人 サンロータス研究所

　　　　〒 170-0004 東京都豊島区北大塚 3-31-3-305
　　　　TEL/FAX 03-5974-2160

印刷・製本 大村紙業

About the Author

Chisako Takeoka (shown speaking on May 30, 2009) was born in Hatchobori, Hiroshima City in February, 1928. A graduate of Yamanaka Girls'High School, on August 6, 1945, she was exposed to the atomic bomb and the "black rain" at her home in Koiuemachi, about three kilometers from the hypocenter. After the bombing, she spent several days walking through the ruins of Hiroshima in search of her mother, a head nurse at an army hospital in Hiroshima.

Joining the Soka Gakkai in 1959, she was active in the Hiroshima Housewives'Alliance for 15 years. Her activities as a peace activist include:

- Editor of "Voices for Posterity – Cries from Hell," a collection of Hiroshima survivor accounts of atomic bomb experiences.
- In June, 1982, participated as a Hiroshima/Nagasaki atomic bomb survivor in the Soka Gakkai's delegation to the UN's 2nd Special Session on Disarmament in New York, where she bore witness to horrors of the bomb and engaged in dialogue with physicists who took part in the Manhattan Project.
- At the request of the Hiroshima Peace Culture Center, went to Volgograd (the former Stalingrad), Russia in 2001 to convey her atomic bomb experience to students at two national universities.
- She is one of the founding members of the witness program at the Peace Memorial Museum, where she has related the account of her atomic bomb experience to visitors for over 20 years.

Hiroshima:
Forging a Mission
from Misfortune

Living as a Witness to the Atomic Bomb

Chisako Takeoka

TRANSLATED FROM
THE JAPANESE
BY
Andrew Clark

Originally published in Japanese as
Hiroshima No Shukumei O Shimei Ni Kaete
by Speakman Shoten.
Copyright © Chisako Takeoka 2010

Published 2014 by Speakman Shoten
2-20-1 Misaki-cho, Chiyoda-ku, Tokyo 101-0061 Japan
© 2014 by Chisako Takeoka
Reprinted 2015

Printed in Japan

Contents

Hiroshima (1946)

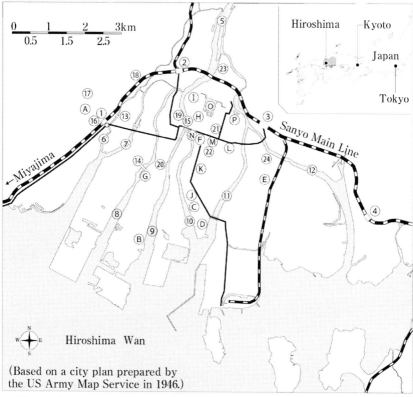

0   1   2   3km
  0.5 1.5 2.5

Hiroshima — Kyoto

Japan

Tokyo

↖ Miyajima

Sanyo Main Line

N W E S

Hiroshima Wan

(Based on a city plan prepared by
the US Army Map Service in 1946.)

(Stations)
① Koi St.
② Yokogawa St.
③ Hiroshima St.
④ Mukainada St.
(Rivers)
⑤ Ōta-gawa
⑥ Yamate-gawa
  /Koi-gawa
⑦ Fukusima-gawa
⑧ Tenma-gawa
⑨ Hon-kawa
⑩ Motoyasu-gawa
⑪ Kyobashi-gawa
⑫ Enko-gawa
(Bridges)
⑬ Koi-bashi

⑭ Kannon-bashi
⑮ Aioi-bashi
(Towns & districts)
⑯ Koimachi
⑰ Koiuemachi
⑱ Yamate-chō
⑲ Takajomachi
⑳ Funairimachi
㉑ Hatchobori
㉒ Shintenchi
㉓ Hakushima-chō
㉔ Danbaramachi
(Schools)
Ⓐ Koi elementary School
Ⓑ Eba elementary School
Ⓒ Yamanaka Girls' School
Ⓓ Shudo Junior & Senior H.S.

Ⓔ Hijiyama Girls' School
(Hospitals)
Ⓕ Shima Hospital
Ⓖ Funairi hospital
Ⓗ 1st Army Hospital
Ⓘ 2nd Army Hospital
Ⓙ Japanese Red Cross
(Other)
Ⓚ Chugoku Elec Pwr Co.
Ⓛ Chugoku News Co.
Ⓜ Fukuya Dept Store
Ⓝ Atomic bomb dome
Ⓞ Hiroshima castle
Ⓟ Shukkei-en

Photo by Kiyotaka Kinoshita（2014）

| **Mariko Higashino** | **Chisako Takeoka** | **Emi Higashino** |
| (Daughter) | (Author) | (Granddaughter) |

Ryō Kunisada (1903–1967)

This photograph is registered in permanent storage in the Victims'Information Area of the second basement in the Hiroshima National Peace Memorial Hall for the Atomic Bomb Victims.

The photo caption simply reads: *"Age at exposure: 42; Place exposed: Hiroshima City Funairi Hospital, Funairi-saiwai-cho Hiroshima-shi (present day Funairi-saiwai-cho, Naka-ku, Hiroshima-shi); Residence: 209-7 Uemachi-ku, Koimachi, Hiroshima-shi; Occupation: Health care worker (head nurse at the Hiroshima First Army Hospital, 15th Area Army, 2nd General Army)."*

Preface to the English edition

The year 2015 marks the 70th anniversary of the end of the Pacific War. It also marks the 70th anniversary of the atomic bombings of the cities of Hiroshima and Nagasaki.

This book is a record of the living hell that resulted from one of those bombings, as seen through my 17-year-old eyes. It also records discovery of a path out of that hell, which I and my family found thanks to Daisaku Ikeda, our mentor in faith and the President of the Soka Gakkai International.

I have received numerous requests asking whether this volume might be published in English.

I witnessed the bombing when I was 17 years old. This year, I turned 87. Providence has granted me a strong constitution. I continue to look after my eighty nine-year-old husband, and am still capable of driving my own car.When asked to do so, I continue to bear witness about my atomic bomb experience to junior and senior high school students, whether they come to Hiroshima during school field trips, or I visit them at schools around the country.

Under a program established by the municipal government of Hiroshima City, a system has been established for training successors to witnesses who are direct survivors of the bombing, making it possible to continue transmitting our experiences into the future. My daughter, Mariko Higashino, has agreed to become the official successor to my own experience.

My granddaughter, Emi Higashino, has also expressed

2

a determination to become an heir in this tradition.

Nothing could make me happier.

I earnestly hope that people of the world, and particularly those in countries that have nuclear weapons, will read this account, and help make sure that Hiroshima and Nagasaki are the last places to suffer the effects of nuclear weapons.

My son Seiji tells me that, according to a 5,000-year-old Egyptian creation myth, the sun was born from the Lotus.

"On the first mound of existence, the myth recounts, there grew a lotus flower. As the bud opened into sweet heady fullness, Re, the sun, emerged from the heart of the flower, bringing first light into the world." *

I sincerely hope that this little book may bloom like the lotus bud and give birth to a sun that illuminates many future generations.

I would like to extend my great gratitude to Yoshiko Kawamura and Andrew Clark for their indispensable assistance in bringing this English edition to publication.

February 3, 2015, Hiroshima
Chisako Takeoka

* 'The Creation According to Re', by Christine El-Mahdy in
"*Mythology: Myths, Legends and Fantasies*" (Alice Mills, editor)

Preface

As the green spring draws to a close, I feel a hint of dampness in the wind. About two weeks ago, my 60-year-old son called from Tokyo, telling me that he will be making a long-overdue visit to Hiroshima, and saying that he would like to hear me talk about my experiences. This request takes me completely by surprise. That was in May of last year (2009).

He says he will be visiting Hiroshima with a friend on Saturday and Sunday, May 30th and 31st. It so happens that I am scheduled to speak to some young people on the 30th at the Hiroshima National Peace Memorial Hall for the Atomic Bomb Victims. I invite my son and his friend to come and listen.

It has now been 30 years since I moved from Koiuemachi on the western edge of town to Takatori in the north. From there, the drive to the Peace Center takes about 30 minutes. The oleander trees, their blossoms just starting to emerge, flow by the car window. I reach the meeting place at the Peace Memorial Park, in what used to be the Nakajima district of Hiroshima, at about 2 in the afternoon. Here, in 30 minutes, I will speak for about an hour to students from Hiroshima Shudo University.

I drop in to the East Building of the Peace Memorial Museum to give my regards to the staff at the Outreach Division, and then head to where the students are waiting. My son has been on my mind all day, and as I walk, I ponder upon what I will talk about, and what I hope to convey. He has never been in the audience before. After wavering about what approach to take, I finally decide to take my

usual direct approach. I will simply tell what happened as accurately as possible, without adornment; that will be best.

I reach the hall about five minutes before the students start coming in, giving me some time to chat with my son and his friend, who arrived earlier. I had been worrying about his health, but he seems to be doing well.

My son and his friend are invited to sit with Professor Morishima, who brought the students, and Principal Kimura of the Hiroshima Peace Culture Center. The two seem a bit surprised by this, but gladly accept. Professor Morishima introduces my son to the students, who are now seated. Then I begin speaking to these youth, all younger than my grandchildren, the sons and daughters of my son and daughter.

"Today, the things I must speak of are dark and sad. They happened when I was only 17, just about your age. On the morning of that day. . . ."

At the suggestion of my son, who heard me speak that day, I determined to write my recollections down as a memoir. In the year and a half since, the days have been filled with nostalgia, pain and sadness, but also with a shining hope. I am grateful to everyone who has given me this opportunity.

October,2010
Chisako Takeoka

1

AUGUST 6

As I begin to speak, I look at the students who have come to hear me talk, and I am deeply moved by their youth; they are all younger than my youngest grandchild.

ॐ

The story I have to tell you today is a dark, dark tale of war. There is nothing bright or pleasant here, nothing happy; only dark, sad, and painful things. I suffer from the heat each summer, and I imagine it is the same for many of you. Since it is supposed to be hot today, please try to make yourselves as comfortable as you can.

As you all know, at 8:15 in the morning on August 6, 1945, an atomic bomb exploded at an altitude of between six and eight hundred meters a little to the east of this Peace Memorial Park, directly above the spot that is now the location of the Shima Geka Hospital.

On the 5th, just one day previously, I was making parts for weapons in the factory of the Toyo Seikan Company, which at the time was a large munitions plant.

Junior high schools at that time were 4-year schools, none of which were coeducational of course, and I was a graduate of a girls' school. Starting in April of 1944, everyone who graduated was immediately required to go to work for the army or the navy. I became a member of the Women's Volunteer Corps. After I graduated, there was no chance to think about going to college or what

to make of myself, or to consider anything personal. The war and its conduct always came first. After the war started, things needed to fulfill the basic needs of people rapidly disappeared. Money, food, and clothing were all taken to fulfill military needs, so there was nothing left for ordinary folk.

I think the conditions we endured are beyond the imagination of today's young people, especially elementary school students. A single pencil was a treasure, and an eraser would of necessity be used until it was a tiny nub. When I was a sixth-grader in elementary school, art supplies were not available, and the only paper we had for drawing pictures was a dark, coarse material that was easily torn. We lived with almost nothing and everyone cooperated to a single end, because "we must win the war."

On the morning of August 5, wearing a headband I had made myself, I was hard at work making parts for weapons. Just like a regular factory worker, I used a large file to smooth the faces of parts. Toward evening we were told, "We have to get these weapons to the battlefield now, or it will be too late. Everyone's got to work through the night tonight." Of course, there were no telephones at the time, so there was no way for us to tell our families that we would not be coming home. It didn't really matter, though, because everyone knew how busy we were, and just assumed we had to stay at work. That's the way things were.

The parts we were making were components for the *Kaiten* ("Heaven Shaker") piloted torpedoes being

8

built at the Kure Naval Arsenal. These suicide weapons, intended to sink large enemy warships at the cost of their pilots'lives, were manned by a single person and measured about 15 meters in length and about one meter in diameter; just about the width of a small desk. Some of the pilots went straight from junior high school to three months of special training, and then were sent into action in these weapons. So many promising young lives scattered to the wind, "for our Country."

We all hated the war, knowing how such weapons were used, and deep in our hearts we did not want to make them. But no one could speak out because they knew the horrific consequences. Anyone who did so would be viewed with suspicion, driven out, and in the end taken away by the police or the army. So we all stayed quiet and worked in silence.

When dawn approached, we were told, "Women's Volunteer Corps members can go home now and rest." This was early in the morning on August 6. Dawn had not yet broken. "Ah, at last. . ." we thought.

They only let the Women's Volunteer Corps go home. We had not rested in two or three months, and in our eagerness, we looked up at the sky as we left the plant. The heavens are incredibly beautiful in the pre-dawn mornings of summer, and this day was especially so, with brilliantly shining stars and not a trace of cloud.

"Looks like it will be a hot one today. It would be great to go to the beach."

But at the time, bathing in the ocean was forbidden, because many swimmers had been killed at the beach near Miyajima by small enemy fighter airplanes called

"Grummans," which would fly low over the water and strafe the bathers. Many were killed in their swimsuits.

"I'd still like to see the ocean."

"Let's go then."

"Yes, let's go!"

So my friends and I, three of us altogether, exchanged promises that we would meet and go to Miyajima.

"Let's go on the train that leaves at 8:15."

At the time, trains bound for Miyajima left from Koimachi at the western edge of Hiroshima. There weren't as many Miyajima-bound trains in those days as the Japan Railways runs now. We pledged we'd meet at Koi Station at 8:15. As we left the factory, we bubbled with anticipation. "This will be great! How wonderful! I'm so glad!"

Since it was still dark, I went home first to our house in Koiuemachi to do laundry and straighten up. My mother was very busy at work, and could not come home every day. Also living with us was my grandmother, who went out for a walk around 7:30, saying she wanted to enjoy the cool morning air. After busily straightening up, I glanced at the wall clock and was startled to see that it was already 8:10.

"Oh no, I'm late! We promised to meet in time for the 8:15, but I'll never make it now. What shall I do?" I hurried to the foyer and took a small mirror out of my pocket to look at my face. At the time I had long hair that I kept in a braid. I was relieved to see that my hair at least was still tidy.

I took another look at the clear, blue sky, then another chance look in the mirror, and it was at that

instant: A flash! And then BOOM.

Ah! My hands flew to my head, and I lost all awareness.

I am not sure how many minutes passed. But when I regained consciousness with a start, I found myself inexplicably lying in an unexpected place. I was on the ground in the middle of a sweet potato patch about thirty meters behind the house.

"What happened?" I thought. Then I remembered the flash and the boom and thought, "My house must have been hit by an incendiary bomb!" At the time, the word "bomb" to me meant an incendiary device. I had no knowledge of other types of bombs. By this point in the war, incendiary bombs had turned Tokyo, Osaka and Okayama into burnt ruins, and I now thought that it was Hiroshima's turn. At the military port of Kure not far from Hiroshima, the air raid siren wailed and incendiaries fell almost every night. But it hadn't suffered any major air raids, even though it was a military port.

"It's an incendiary bomb! An incendiary bomb has fallen on our house!"

When an incendiary bomb falls, it hisses for a while, and then bursts into flame. When that happened, we would immediately throw water on the bomb and run away. We were all drilled in this repeatedly, so buckets of water for extinguishing fires were placed at various points around the house.

"Oh! Nothing's burning yet, so if I act quickly, I might be in time!"

I thought I should go into the house and thrown water on the bomb. The problem was, I couldn't stand

up. I couldn't understand why my legs didn't work, and didn't know what to do. There also seem to be something strange about my head, so I reached up and touched it. To my surprise, it was bleeding. Thinking something had hit me, I glanced up at the sky.

There a sight was unfolding, unlike anything I'd ever seen before; a roiling, dark, gray-black mass was rapidly spreading over the sky. It was awful, sickening. At the time I couldn't tell whether it was smoke or a cloud, but now I know that it was the radiation-filled mushroom cloud of the atomic bomb. At the time, no one knew. Sick with horror, I could only think about getting into my house as soon as possible.

Crawling over the ground, I finally reached it and went inside. I saw that the stairway to the second floor was knocked askew, and couldn't tell where anything was. Somehow I managed to search the first and second floors, but I couldn't find any bomb, or hear any noise.

"That's funny," I thought, "Maybe it wasn't an incendiary bomb." So I went back outside, and found all of my neighbors coming out into the street. There was a lady, bleeding from a large, triangular piece of glass embedded in her back. Another lady had a piece of corroded sheet metal sticking out of her bleeding side, like a big, rusty nail. The people who had been indoors were all severely injured, and came out in the streets covered with blood.

"Oh, those poor ladies! Those wounds must be treated right away, or they'll become infected. We've got to remove the glass and nails, stop the bleeding, and apply disinfectant." But there was no medicine, or any

disinfectant. We still had running water, though; that never stopped. All we could do was wash their wounds with running tap water and stop the bleeding. Since there was no medicine, we had all been taught how to stop bleeding by people who did it for a living.

"Please take care of the bleeding. I'll go down to the main road and see what's happening," I said, and I went down to the road, which was a short distance away. As I got up to move, my own grandmother came hurrying back from her walk. I was so relieved to see her safe. She had been walking beside the river that flowed near the Koi national school, and by chance was under a bridge when the bomb exploded. The bridge sheltered her from the blast.

My home in Koi town was just three kilometers to the west of the hypocenter, the point over which the bomb exploded. Almost everyone within a two-kilometer radius of that point was killed instantly. Those that weren't mostly died within a few hours, maybe three, or six at most.

The city of Hiroshima is laid out roughly in a circle, and sits in a river delta which is surrounded by mountains on three sides. The terrain is such that, given a clear day and sunny skies for aiming, an attack with even a single atomic weapon cannot fail. During the thirty minutes starting at about 8 a.m., the wind shifts from the mountains to the sea, so the air is calm during this time. I didn't know about this thirty-minute period of calm, even though I grew up in Hiroshima. But the American military knew, and had taken it into account in their detailed planning for that morning's attack.

Many important Japanese army facilities were located within the two-kilometer radius. The conditions guaranteed their destruction, as well as the deaths of everyone living in the area. From the point of view of the American military planners, Hiroshima offered the best conditions for an attack amongst those cities that had not yet been destroyed by air raids. The Ōta River flows into the city from the north, dividing into several branches in the delta. There were seven such branches at the time, but the two on the west have been combined into one stream, so now there are six. The city is also close to the ocean.

Koi town, just three kilometers from the city center, was a quiet, bucolic place, nestled against the mountains. During summer, the air was filled with fireflies. From Koi Station, now called Nishi-Hiroshima, our house was about a ten-minute walk up a gentle slope from the station in the direction of the mountains, away from the sea.

I went to the road that goes down that slope and looked in the direction of the ocean. "What's that?" There was a strange black mass advancing slowly up the slope. "What on earth could it be?" As I wondered, the black mass came closer and closer.

Then I saw that it was a crowd of people. They were all blackened and severely injured. The women's hair was all disarrayed, and burnt skin was hanging loose from their bodies. It looked like seaweed that has just been dragged from the sea. Their skin, burnt and festering, peeling away from their shoulders and down their arms, hung from their fingers. It was a whole group of such people.

14

"It's so hot, please help!"

"Mommy, it hurts!"

"Sister, my throat hurts!"

"Brother, I want water!"

"My throat hurts! Water, give me water!"

All the while calling the names of people in their families, they cried, "It's hot! It's hot! Water! Water!" It was a terrible thing to behold. Near the road was a large house, and the roof of that house was intact, so many people tried to crowd into it to shelter from the burning sun, but as they did, others were collapsing in the middle of the road by the dozens.

I stopped thinking consciously. I rushed frantically about, as if in a dream. I would tap severely burned people on the shoulder, telling them, "Hang in there! Don't die!" "You did great to make it here, are you alone? Where did you come from? What's your name?"

They'd all been calling out to each other a moment ago, but now they were silent. The burns had cooked their throats on the inside.

"I know you can't talk or say your name, but you made it this far, so you'll be OK now, hang in there!"

More of the neighborhood ladies were coming out in the street. "Oh my, how awful, this is terrible, we have to help them. What can we do? We've got to get some medicine on those burns!" But there wasn't any medicine anywhere. All we could do was wash their burns with water. We wanted to feed them, too; given something to eat, they could gain energy and perhaps live. But there wasn't much in the way of food to give them either. Food was rationed, and distribution was running a week late.

All we'd had for breakfast was water, nothing to eat.

We had to do something, but what? "Water, give me water!", the burned crowd cried again and again, so again and again we opened the faucets and brought water for them to drink, to cool their burns, to wipe them clean. But often we couldn't really wipe them, because their burns were so bad that wiping was out of the question. The only towels we had were called "Japan towels" and they were nothing more than pieces of cloth. Even so, we didn't have enough of them. All we could do was dip the towels we had in water and put them on people's chests, or gently put them on their heads.

A little time passed, and it started to get dark, as if the sun was going down. "What's happening?" I thought. "It's still morning, isn't it?" "Yes, still morning. . . ." I didn't have a watch, so it was hard to be sure of the time. "It's still morning." "That's right, still morning," we assured each other as our surroundings grew darker and darker. And that's when a dark, inky rain began to fall, pounding down in a deluge. It was the "black rain."

When the bomb exploded, it sucked up people, houses, dust and all sorts of matter in its updraft, and this matter coalesced into dark, black clouds that flowed to the northwest. Koimachi, the place where I lived, was right in the path of this cloud. That awful dark, sickening whirlpool that I had seen while lying in the yam patch had changed into a cloud, and was now releasing its burden on as coal black rain.

"Ohhh, this is sickening. Everyone, please come in under the canopy." But the people lying out in the road couldn't move, and the black rain pounded down on

them. The black droplets stuck to our arms and feet in big, round gobs, about the side of a soy bean, and couldn't be removed by wiping or washing with water.

As time passed, true evening approached. It was about then that one of the people approached and, standing in front of me, called me by name, "Chii-chan." I was startled. She called me by name. She was charred black all over, and I had no idea who she was. Her head was charred too, and as I got closer, I could see some crispy object stuck in her hair. It was all muddied with the black rain, and blood was flowing out of her split cheeks. Looking closer, I could see that she had countless small holes in her chest and back. Blood was oozing out of all of them.

"Dear, you've been badly hurt. Ah! You're Hoko-chan (Mihoko), aren't you? I'm so glad you survived. How did you ever make it up here?"

Although we had no medicine or food, I took her into the house and soothed her injuries with water as best I could. She was one of the girls I had promised to meet at Koi Station to go to Miyajima. She lived out beyond Hiroshima's Tenma-cho, and had been riding a streetcar to Koi that morning when the bomb exploded, blowing her out the tram window. That much she could remember, but what happened next she said was a blank. When she came to, she was lying in the river. From the tram stop to the river was over a kilometer, and she had been blown there in an instant by the fierce force of the blast wave, which travelled at a rate of two or three hundred meters per second.

"I'm so glad you're alive, so glad. . . ."

There was a small room next to the one we occupied, and happening to glance that way, I caught a glimpse of something black moving. "That's strange," I thought, "I thought there was no one here but Grammy and me, has someone else come in?" And when I went to look there were thirteen people, all of them burned black. They all writhed with the excruciating pain that consumed their bodies. Trying to ease the pain even a bit, they were rubbing their arms together with the person next to them.

"Everyone, you all did great to make it here. I'll bring you some water right away. It's OK now." And I gave water to each one, although half of them weren't breathing any more. I wanted to feed the ones who were living, but there was nothing to eat.

"What's your name?" ... Ah, I thought, if they can't speak, I'll bring pencil and paper so they can write their names. But when I tried to get them to hold the pencil, I saw that the bones of their fingers were melted and the flesh was peeling off, so holding a pencil was impossible. Then their eyes became gradually still. Perhaps their ears couldn't hear, either. I hoped to find out their names at least, by whatever means, but it was not to be. I felt enormous dismay. After making it all this way, at least I wanted to learn their names.

Then I thought, if this many people have come up toward the mountain, what can it be like inside the city? "Everyone, I'm going to go up the mountain to take a look. Don't you die while I'm gone!" And I headed for the hill at the back of the house. At the time, everyone played outdoors, and the place I was headed was where

children would sit on a straw mat and slide down the hill from midway up. I climbed up to the top of that hill.

When I got there, downtown Hiroshima was clearly visible in the faint light of evening. There was almost nothing left. A chill ran down my spine. About a third of the Chugoku Newspaper Company's reinforced concrete building was still there, and there was a bit of the Fukuya Department Store still standing; just about everything else was a burnt and festering wasteland. In all of downtown Hiroshima, home and workplace to tens of thousands of people until just that morning, there was not a building left standing. It was totally destroyed.

My insides churned as I realized this could not be the work of incendiary bombs. I realized then that some enormous weapon must have been used. Thinking that, my eyes turned toward Aioi bridge. This was the largest bridge in Hiroshima, and is situated a little to the north of today's Peace Memorial Park. I could see Aioi bridge, and I could see the river. Although I couldn't see the water, it was easy to tell the river was there. Looking more to the east, there was an army hospital on a large site close to Hiroshima castle and Gokoku shrine.

"Ohhhh, help, it's all burned. Mother! Please be alive!"

My mother was a medical worker at the army hospital, the head nurse. The hospital was a place that took in wounded soldiers returning from overseas. Tending to them constantly, she hadn't been home in a week. But there was nothing left in the area of the hospital. Oh, mother!

"I will come looking for you in the morning, please

don't die!"

So early in the morning on the 7th, I waited for dawn and, leaving our home in the care of my grandmother, set off alone for Hiroshima. On my head I wore a soaking wet air-raid hood, and my feet were covered in a pair of ragged shoes. It was a time when a pair of shoes had to last for many years. It wasn't only that we had no money; there just weren't any shoes to buy. So every tear would be mended, and when that tore, a piece of cloth would be affixed over the tear. The soles would have two or three holes, and the inside of the shoes would become sopping wet if they were worn outdoors in the rain. But I was going into the midst of fires, and thought that any shoes would be better than going barefoot. So I put them on, slung a canteen full of water over my shoulder and left the house.

I went down the hill from Koiuemachi, which is up against the mountain, to the town of Koi below. Koi is located about three kilometers from the hypocenter across from the city on the western side of a large river, and had not been exposed to flying sparks. So it did not burn. Still, many houses had been crushed by the blast wave, and those that were still standing were knocked a-kilter. I could heard women's voices crying, "Help! I'm in here!" from beneath the crushed buildings. But those voices got fainter and fainter. People were calling for help right in front of me, and even though the buildings weren't burning, there was nothing I could do to help them.

At the time, just about the only people remaining in the country were young children, school students, old men

and women, and women without much bodily strength. Getting people out of the wreckage meant lifting lots of heavy beams, but since no one had eaten much recently, they didn't have the strength. So the voices just became fainter and fainter, and they couldn't be helped. So many women died this piteous death.

Leaving that place, I crossed Koi-bashi. I went to the next river. The bridge was half destroyed and couldn't be crossed. That was a small wooden bridge. It was a place we liked to play when swimming was allowed, and we were permitted to swim in the river. We liked to wait for the tide to come in, and would jump into the river from the parapets. That dear, old wooden bridge had been washed half away. "OK!" I thought, and decided to swim. I'd made it about half way across when I saw the bodies of several women drifting downstream, half sinking, half floating. I thought, "One of them might be mother," and hastily paddled in that direction, but found that they all had long hair. None of them could be my mother; she cut her hair short because of her work.

Leaving them, I climbed up onto the remaining part of the bridge that extended from the opposite bank. Although I was just a 17-year-old girl, I knew the bridge well and had no trouble climbing up. Finally getting across the river, I headed for the city center. I crossed the next bridge and the next, and after the third reached the factory where the Women's Volunteer Corps worked. It had been knocked completely flat by the blast, and there was machine oil burning everywhere. "I wonder what became of the factory workers who stayed after the Women's Volunteer Corps left yesterday morning. If

we'd kept working, I guess I'd be dead, too." I thought there still might be someone there who needed help, so I wandered around the large factory looking. But there was no one to be seen. There was just me, wandering around in my air-raid hood.

There were no people to be seen anywhere. Perhaps they fled in a safe direction, I thought. I made my way closer and closer to the city center, wondering where they might have gone as I finally reached Aioi bridge. Then I glanced at the river. Because of its nearness to the sea, the water level rose and fell with the tides. It was now just high tide. But, I couldn't see any water in the river. Both upstream and downstream, as far as I could see, the stream was crammed with corpses, rafts of floating dead.

I stared in horror. This was not the result of incendiary bombs. It had to be something much, much larger. Trying to suppress a growing shiver, I repeatedly called "Oh, Mother! Mother!" to the river of floating corpses, but of course there was no answer. How in the world would I ever find her? I thought of looking for a boat. Then I thought, no, a boat would do no good. There were so many corpses floating in the river that a boat wouldn't be able to move. If I could find anyone walking, anyone at all, I would have asked them to help me. But no matter how much I searched, there was no one else alive there but me.

Looking at the corpses that floated nearest, I saw that they were burned all over their bodies. The pain they felt must have been unimaginable, as well as their desire for water. They had jumped into the river because there was nothing else they could do. Leaping in one after

another, they drank the river water and died. They were all horribly swollen. With heads and faces swollen up like beach balls, there was no way to distinguish one person from the next.

I was at a complete loss. I had no idea how I was going to find my mother. The only person alive and walking about was me. Setting off upstream on foot along the top of the embankment, I could see the round roof of the Industrial Promotion Hall across the river, standing there like the corpse of a building. Looking further up, I saw three men, all totally naked, pulling corpses out of the river. Oh, I thought, that's the site of the army hospital. I hurried over, thinking that they might know something of my mother if I asked.

About half way across Aioi bridge, I came across three people lying in the road, all burned completely black. Running over, I shook them and tried to offer encouragement, but their eyes were open only a sliver, and not moving at all. I imagine they died some hours previously; there was nothing I could do for them. The parapets of Aioi bridge were made of stone, but they had all been knocked down; not even one remained. Finally crossing the bridge, I came to where the three men were working.

They looked startled at the sight of me, saying "Sister! Where did you come from? You're not burned!" and "You're wearing clothes!" They seemed to think that was very strange.

"Yes, I came here from the hilltop in Koi to look for my mother."

"I see! So your mother's a nurse at the army

hospital? In that case, she might not be alive any more. There were hundreds here until this morning, but they all died one after another with blood pouring out of their mouths, noses and ears."

"There's a group of forty or fifty that are still living, but it's impossible to tell who they are, and they are so weak that it's just a matter of time until they die. I'm afraid there's little chance that your mother is still alive." They said she was no doubt floating in the river or buried under the hospital, and told me, "Sister, you should go back to Koi right away."

"You at least must live. If the enemy planes come, you'll be completely exposed here, and they'd shoot you in an instant. Go home now!"

I told them I would, but as I turned to go back, they called out and stopped me. "Sister, since you've come all this way, you might as well look at the bodies that are lined up here. Your mother might be among them." But all of the people were so badly disfigured, it was impossible to tell them apart.

"Did your mother have some feature you could identify her by?"

"No, nothing that I can think of."

"Think again. There must be something."

"Oh, I know. My mother had three gold teeth."

Thinking to check their teeth, I picked up a piece of wood and opened the mouths of 5, 10, 30, 40 corpses to look. Their mouths did not open easily. Through their swollen lips, I could only see in about three centimeters. They were so disfigured that they did not seem human.

"Well sister, did you find anything? Anyone with gold

teeth?"

"No, no one."

"That's what I thought. You'd better hurry home now."

The three were medics, army medics from the hospital. They had suffered only light burns and injuries, and wanting to do something, they were pulling bodies from the river. They hoped that sooner or later their efforts might be rewarded if even one or two people searching for lost family could be reunited with their loved ones.

I left them to their work and went back the way I'd come, once again crossing Aioi bridge. Then I headed for my aunt's house, which was close to a place called Takajomachi. The house was in a place located 500 meters from the hypocenter. At the time, my aunt was living there with a 4th-year female student attending the national school.

I went to where I thought the house must be, looked around, and found a cistern with her family name written on it in charcoal. "This is the place!" At just past eight in the morning, I thought they probably would have been in the living room drinking water, even though there was nothing to eat. I located the spot in the wreckage where I thought the living room might be and began to dig. I dug using the tips of my shoes. The rubble and stones were still hot, and I burned the tips of my feet.

Digging on and on, at last I found a familiar-looking stone gatepost, and removing the rocks and rubble from the area of the living room, I found a small patch of cloth. It was a piece of my aunt's clothes. Digging in the

surrounding area, at last I found the two, who had died sitting, facing each other. There was nothing left but bones. The skulls were sitting on the pelvic bones.

The heat of the bomb was unimaginable. The temperature of the sun's surface is 8,000 degrees Celsius. They say that, at the 600-meter altitude where it exploded, the bomb's fireball reached a temperature of 6,000 degree Celsius, and when the fireball reached the ground, it was still 4,000 degrees. Exposed to temperatures like that, nothing could survive. There would be no time to run away, or even to think of doing so. I am glad that I found them. They would have wanted me to find their bones. The people floating in the river were so disfigured that there was no way they could ever be identified.

I quietly put my hands together for the two, and then picked up a few of their bones and wrapped them carefully in a handkerchief. As I left my aunt's place to return home, the air raid sirens began wailing. I had heard the sirens starting up in the east, and now they were overhead. I had to hide somewhere, but there was no place to hide nearby. Off in the distance, I saw a large, half-crumpled cistern. I thought of going there and crouching down. Crouching would still leave me visible from the sky, but thinking that the cistern might offer some protection if bombs were dropped, I ran to it on my burned feet and tried to make myself small.

Then I glanced down and was startled to see someone beneath me. It was a young mother, who had died holding her baby. Holding her baby to her breast, she had fled here trying to protect it, and reaching the

spot had died. The baby's two feet were visible beneath the mother's charred, dangling flesh. They were clean and not burned. The left foot had some glass embedded in it, and I thought that it might have been taking a nap in some sheltered spot in their home when the mother pulled it out and brought it here.

Thinking the baby might be alive, I pulled it out and held it to my breast. But it was not breathing, and its body was cold. Holding the cold, lifeless body in my arms, at that moment I returned to myself. It was the first time that I ever realized what it means "to return to one's self." Up to that point, everything had seemed dreamlike, and I wasn't even truly aware of who I was. From the previous day, with trying to help all the burned people, setting out to look for my mother, finding the river full of floating corpses, I hadn't had any room left for thinking.

As I held the cold baby to my breast, I began to tremble and cry in anger. Helplessly, I wept, my tears flowing on and on. Why, why did even this poor, innocent baby have to die? The rage swelled within me, as I thought, "Ahh, who started this stupid war! I will never forgive them! America, Japan, it doesn't matter, I will never forgive any of them!"

I couldn't bring myself to leave that mother and her child for a long time, but finally wrestled a measure, bade them farewell, and returned to our house in Koi.

When I got home, five of my aunts were there, having come by way of the mountain road. Two of them were barely breathing, and died shortly after I gave them some water. The other three were somehow hanging on.

I went out again to look for my mother the next day, August 8. The previous day, I'd turned left after crossing Aioi bridge, so today I decided to search for mother in the area on the right. The area to the right was where Hiroshima's main shopping district was located. First I found twenty or thirty people lying in the road, all of them burned completely black. They were all dead, and there was no one to look after them. I checked them all to see if mother was among them. Not this one, no, not this one either. . . oh, this might be her. . . no, it's not. At that moment I noticed some street rats. They had probably survived in the river bed, and now were feeding on the corpses. "Oh," I thought, "how pathetic." This is what happens to people in war.

My emotions seething, I wandered to the south, and after a while found myself standing in the burned ruins next to the Japanese Red Cross hospital. There, human remains had been piled into mountains. Human corpses were stacked for cremation. Two of these mountains were on fire. A third was just about to be torched. "Wait a moment, please," I said. "I came to look for my mother." And I walked all around the mountain, trying to see whether my mother was there, No matter how much I looked, none of the bodies had recognizable features, so I just couldn't be sure. "Oh, mother, I'm so sorry. I couldn't find you today, either." And with that sad lump in my chest, I went home.

When I got home, there was a message waiting. Not far away stood the Koi national school, surrounded by beautiful greenery. The message said that large holes had been dug in the school yard, and that people should bring

the dead. In the houses knocked a-kilter, there were still many people who had just died, or who had died the day before. All these poor, nameless souls were carried to the school yard. There, surrounded by the beauty of nature, about 2,000 people were cremated.

It was truly a horrendous spectacle, and once again I felt a burgeoning rage as I thought, "Who could imagine such a thing? Oh, this war must come to an end!"

The next day was the 9th, and this time I turned to search the area around Kannon bridge in the south. Looking down on the river from the buckled bridge, I saw a floating body wrapped in a blanket. It was a woman, but I could see from the long hair drifting in the water that it was not my mother. I didn't find her. From about noon that day I started feeling woozy and nauseous. My aunts that were taking refuge at our house were also weighing on my mind, so I went home without further ado. Their burns and other wounds were severe. Pus was coming out of the wounds, and the smell was permeating the house. The wounds were infested with maggots.

I went out on the 10th to look some more, but my body just wouldn't cooperate. I was very shaky, and when I walked, I felt queasy in my chest. When I put my hands to my head that night, it was throbbing with pain. There was no medicine for pain, and when I put my hands to my head again, they came away covered in hair that had fallen out of my scalp. At this revolting development, I looked closer at my arms and saw that both of them were disfigured with three or four purplish spots, each about the size of a small egg. I was becoming sick, and thought that I might die. "Oh mother, I'm so

sorry! I might not be able to look for you tomorrow." But in my heart I cried, "Please be alive. If you're alive, I promise I will find you."

That evening, old Takagi came to visit from the big farm house where he lived nearby.

"Chii-chan, I hear you've been looking for your mother every day, but haven't been able to find her. Are you going to look again tomorrow?"

"No, I don't think I'll be able to go tomorrow. I'm not feeling well, I'm getting strange purple spots, and my hair is falling out. I feel sick, and I don't think I'll be able to go out."

But old Takagi persisted, "I see. Well, your mother might still be alive and waiting for you to come and get her. Pull yourself up and go look for her. Tomorrow, this old man will go with you, so let's leave in the morning."

So on the next day, August 11, I waited for dawn and then set out again, this time heading for the western part of the city. I had already covered the downtown area centered on Hiroshima Station. As we headed to the west, we encountered an old gentleman.

"Are you two looking for someone?" he asked. "If so, follow the river down toward the sea. Some people have been taken into the national school at Eba." He said there were many dead and dying at the school in Eba.

Heading there as fast as we could, we reached the school and found the corridors crammed with corpses, so many that it was hard to walk among them. The dead were piled five and six deep in haphazard stacks pointing in every which direction. The dead were mostly

undistinguishable, and though we checked them all, turning over those who faced down, we recognized no one. Six days had passed, and now the wounds of even the living were starting to rot. The extreme stench inside the school made breathing almost impossible. Both the living and the dead were black with flies.

Old Takagi went to all the classrooms of the school, calling out mother's name in each. No one in any room spoke or lifted a hand in response. We reached the last room. We'd decided to head home if we found nothing here. Here and there in the classroom, desks had been pushed together, and bodies living or dead had been placed atop them.

I stood by the people who were on the desks at the very front of the room. Old Takagi raised his voice and called out mother's name to everyone there.

"Oy, Ryō-san! Chii-chan is looking for you! If Ryō-san is here, please answer me!"

Maybe in reaction to old Takagi's shout, a head moved slightly on one of the people nearby. Then I heard a tiny voice.

"Chii-chan . . ."

It was my mother! Together, old Takagi and I gently straightened out mother's bent legs, and as we did so, a nurse's uniform appeared from amongst the flies. Yes, it was mother! Her entire head was completely covered in bandages. Someone had given her care. I loosened the bandage around her mouth, looked inside, and there were three gold teeth. Now I was sure, it was mother!

She was burned black all over, and was covered in crusted blood. But it was mother! Wanting to check

further, I pulled slightly at her nurse's uniform. As I did so, hundreds of maggots fell away from her body. It was a miserable, spine-freezing sight. But my mother was alive!

Old Takagi brought two tomatoes out of his pocket. He was a farmer, and he'd brought them to give to my mother in case we found her. She had eaten nothing in six days, and now she slowly ate the tomatoes. "There's no dying for you now, woman. I'm coming for you in the morning with a cart, so you keep on living, hear?" And with that, old Takagi headed back to Koi.

I spend that night with my mother in the school at Eba, calling to her, "Mother! Mother!" and picking flies off of her body, one fly at a time. They were big flies, and being firmly stuck my mother's flesh, were very hard to remove. When I pulled hard with my fingers, mother's loose, burned flesh would come off dangling from theflies' mouths. Removing all of the flies took over two hours. Once done, I reexamined my mother's body, and was shocked again at what I found. Her right side was burned black, and the skin was hanging loose from extensive burns. She had pulled herself out of the fire from beneath the rubble, only gradually working her way to the outside. Splinters of glass were embedded all over the left side of her body.

Old Takagi came to back early the next morning. Together, we loaded mother onto his large cart and at last took her home. The neighborhood ladies all came out in the street to greet us when we arrived. "Thank goodness, she's alive." We took her into our lopsided house and began her treatment. One lady started to take the bandages off my mother's head, then she yelped and

froze. Wondering what it was, I apprehensively took the bandages away and was stunned. My mother's right eyeball was hanging loose from its socket, her face was peppered with shards of embedded glass, and her nose was broken, with bone exposed in two places at the top and bottom. It was all she could do to breathe.

The day we brought mother home was August the 12th, and on that day we took her to the Koi national school to have her examined. Hundreds of wounded were there, and we waited four hours for our turn. We had re-bandaged her head, leaving her mouth uncovered so that she could breathe. The doctor who looked at mother was tired, and when he removed her bandage and saw the dangling eye, he sucked in his breath. He was an internist, not a surgeon, and the only treatment he could provide was to apply some ointment and have a nurse reapply the bandage. The whole process was over in minutes. There were still many people behind us waiting for their turn.

On our way home after leaving the school, mother said, "That was Dr. Doi's voice." I was stunned. Dr. Doi was my father, who I had not seen in a long time, and thought to myself, "that can't be."

After getting mother home, I immediately headed back to the school, but another doctor had already taken over from the one that looked at mother.

I asked where the previous doctor was staying, and was told it was at the Iwahara house, the home of a large land owner. The Iwahara family had a daughter, Hide-chan, who was one class ahead of me at the Yamanaka Girls'High School. I ran into Hide-chan as I was heading for her house.

"Is Dr. Morito Doi staying at your home?", I asked her. "Yes, he was. A truck just came with a new doctor, and Dr. Doi left on that truck," she told me.

"Dr. Doi is my father," I told her.

"What?! If only I'd known. I could have stopped him!" she said.

My mother was in such a hideous state, and the confusion was so great, that my father hadn't recognized her. My father had been working as a doctor in the town of Kami-Ifuku in Okayama, but at the recommendation of his closest friend had moved to Tadanoumi, a town in Hiroshima Prefecture located midway between Takehara and Mihara on the Kure line. With Hiroshima in ruins, doctors had been dispatched to the city from rural areas, and my father had come to the Koi national school with a nurse to treat the injured on the 12th. Two months later, I went by myself to Tadanoumi to see my father, and when I told him of this he was stunned.

Six days I'd searched for my mother, and after finally finding and bringing her home, I had practically nothing for her to eat. We had not even a single grain of rice. Conditions were such that we were truly thankful to still have running water. But unless I did something, I wouldn't be able to feed her, much less get treatment for her injuries. As I agonized over this, an old fellow passing by gave me some timely advice. He said to take her to the village of Hesaka, which was located on the opposite side of the city. "Take your mother to the school there as quickly as you can," he said. He told me that the army hospital's department of medicine had been evacuated to the Hesaka school. He said that there was medicine and

food at the school, as well as doctors and nurses.

Taking his advice, I took mother there in a bicycle-drawn cart. Making our way through the burned ruins of the city took a long time, but after three hours of pedaling, we finally made it to the Hesaka school. When we got there, a soldier came out and said, "This is no good. You've brought an injured person?" He said that there had been army doctors and nurses there, but that they'd all recently died, vomiting blood as they expired. The only one left was a veterinarian. It was this veterinarian that looked at my mother's eye. He said that he would perform surgery immediately to remove it.

Spreading a straw mat on the floor of the classroom, four surviving army medics held down my mother's body as the veterinarian stood on the right side of her face. At that moment, my mother opened her left eye and shouted at the veterinarian: "Please stop! I absolutely do not want this surgery!"

Being not only a nurse, but a head nurse, I believe she was able to tell what sort of operation the veterinarian had in mind simply by looking at him. Being 17 years old, I also knew. There was no anesthetic or other supplies. Looking at the veterinarian's right hand, all he was holding was a small scalpel. With this single scalpel, he was going to cut my mother's right eye from her living flesh. Ah! What should I do?

Then the veterinarian slowly explained. The intense light entering my mother's right eye had caused it to burst out of its socket. However, inside the socket, it was still connected. The veterinarian explained that, if the eye was not removed, mother would also lose the sight in her

left eye.

I gave everything I had to entreating her to accept. "Mother, Hiroshima is totally destroyed, and there is not a single physician left in the city. If you don't have the operation now, you will go blind in your left eye. Be brave . . . I'm sure it will turn out OK!"

During the operation, I went to the corridor outside the classroom to wait until it was over. I endured the sounds of my mother moaning, thrashing about, and screaming with downcast eyes. In my heart, I prayed, "Please, please help my mother." How much time passed, I don't know, but dusk came as the sun went down. A medic came out and told me that the operation was over.

"It's done. Rest here tonight, then take her home tomorrow morning."

But when I took mother home, I had another problem. She did not want to enter our crooked house. She was afraid of being caught in the house in case of another bombing. My mother was severely burned, and her eye had been cut from her bleeding flesh. She wailed with the pain that consumed her from head to toe. Lying down and holding still gave no relief from her pain. At the same time, purple spots were appearing all over my own body, my hair was falling out of my head, and my nausea went on and on.

My only thought then was that this was truly a living hell. Both my mother and I were living in hell. This living hell was something that must never be experienced again by any person of any nation. Wars like this must never again be allowed to occur.

By now, we knew that it was an atomic bomb.

The use of such a horrible weapon, one that would instantaneously snuff out the lives of 200,000 people, was not to be forgiven. If the war was to be lost, then let the end come quickly! The sooner we lost, I thought, the more would be spared. And I determined that someday I would go to America and try to convey to its people the extent of the bomb's devastation.

The entire country was without food, with nothing left. The survivors had nothing to look forward to. It was truly a piteous situation.

2

AFTER THE WAR

I n 1945, my mother, Ryō Kunisada (born in April, 1903, and then 42 years old) worked as the head nurse at the 1st Army Hospital in Hiroshima. I was her only child, and was born to her and my father, Morito Doi (eighteen years her senior) on February 3, 1928. My father was an internist at a hospital in Okayama.

On that August 6th, I thought my mother was working at the army hospital in Hiroshima, which was located less than one kilometer (1,100 yards) from the hypocenter. Crossing Koi-bashi bridge to reach the city, I spent days trying to find her in the areas to the north and east of the hospital. So why was my mother found at the school in Eba, a district to the south of the army hospital on a narrow strip of land that lies between the Tenma and Honkawa rivers?

The reason was that she had been sent to work temporarily at the Funairi hospital, which is located close to Eba. One of the patients at the hospital was a regimental commander's wife. She had taken a turn for the worse, and on the day before the bombing, it was found that she had contracted a communicable disease. Since the Funairi hospital was equipped with an isolation ward, it was decided that the commander's wife should be moved there, and because my mother was the head nurse, she was assigned to accompany the commander's wife. They left the army hospital for Funairi early on the morning of the 6th.

After seeing the wife into her sickroom bed, my

mother went to the office to get a newspaper to read to her. As air raid sirens faded away in the distance, she looked up at the sky through the half-open office window, thinking what a fine day it was. At that moment, the bomb exploded, and its fierce light lanced through her right eye. The fragments that pierced the left side of my mother's face were pieces of glass from the office window.

The severe bomb-related ailments that afflicted my mother required many years of treatment. After her right eye was removed, treatment began with the severe burns on her right side and removal of the shards of glass embedded in her left side. These shards were buried deeply in her flesh, not just in the surface of her skin. Over twenty splinters were removed from her face alone. The number of shards embedded in her entire body was unimaginable.

I am amazed that my mother was able to cope with the terrible pain that she had to endure at the beginning of this ordeal. Her "treatment" was being conducted in Hiroshima, which had been totally destroyed by the bomb. There was no medicine. At first, her treatment consisted of my mother drawing on all of her experience as a nurse to tell me what to do: How to treat the wounds, how to apply bandages and poultices, and how to relieve pain. I learned this all from my mother.

While I was attending girls' school, I worked hard at my studies because I wanted to work in medical care like my mother, and to become a doctor like my father. Although the path to medical school was closed to me by the war, in learning how to deal with mother's injuries under her guidance, I feel that my wish was fulfilled.

It was the wish of a little girl who grew up in various households of relatives who looked after me soon after I was born.

I was born in Hatchobori, the commercial district of Hiroshima. At that time, my mother belonged to a nursing agency and was constantly going to different places to work. My mother's younger brother ran a glass shop in Hatchobori. It was he who looked after me at first. Then it was my mother's older brother in Danbara, where I lived with my aunt and uncle. My uncle was an assistant official at Hiroshima Station, and Danbara was connected to the city by good transportation.

My uncle and his wife had no children of their own. I was born with a weak constitution, and suffered from pneumonia in the winter. I believe this was partly due to the sense of insecurity that I had from being away from my mother while living with my relatives. They treated my pneumonia by applying boiled mustard to my chest and filling the room with steam. I got pneumonia so many times that my aunt told my mother that she should take me somewhere else, as I would certainly suffer from lung disease even if I did not die. In those days, lung disease was regarded as a troublesome and incurable ailment.

My relatives all got together and had a conference. An acquaintance of my father's ran a large hospital in Okayama. As that acquaintance had no children, my relatives decided that I should go there. And so, my uncle and my mother took me to Okayama.

I had large eyes and pale skin from being indoors all the time, yet it seems those people thought I was cute. They took to me right away. I was then three years old.

They said that they would take good care of me, and since they ran a hospital, they had the means to give me treatment. But after leaving me there, on the way to the station my mother had a change of heart. She went back to the hospital and took me away with her. She asked those people to forgive her and forget about me, saying that no matter how poor we were, and no matter what hardships we must endure, she could not let me go and would raise me herself.

My mother asked my grandmother Naka to come to Hiroshima from her farm in Toyoda district. She rented a house in Danbara, and my mother continued working as a nurse while my grandmother took care of me. With my weak constitution, I didn't start attending school until midway through the first year. But, on a ten-point scale, all my marks were eights and nines. My uncle, the assistant railroad official, had attended to my education well, even when I did not attend school.

During my second year, my uncle was transferred from Hiroshima Station to Miyajima Station. The place had sea, mountains, and clean air, and everyone thought that the environment would be good for my health even in winter, so it was decided that I should go there and live with them.

Although there was an elementary school on the mainland, they also thought that riding a boat would be good for me, and so they decided that I would attend elementary school on Itsukushi Island.

Life at Miyajima turned out to be therapeutic, and my condition improved considerably. The child of a family that ran an old lodge on the island was the class leader,

and since I was viewed as the daughter of the assistant manager of Miyajima Station, I became the assistant leader. That was how things were done in those days.

The following year, when I was a 3rd-grader, we moved to Ōhata, a town located across from Yashiro Island in Yamaguchi prefecture.

My uncle was transferred to different stations every year. At his post in Ōhata, my school was located on a hilltop. That was the only elementary school in the area, so life in Ōhata required a lot of walking, and I got stronger and stronger. Official housing for the national railway in Ōhata was located right next to the ocean. It was a place where sea bream were plentiful, and children could fill up a bucket with *gizami* (a kind of wrasse) in about an hour. Coming from out of town, I was a curiosity at the school. All the other children wore straw sandals and *kasuri* kimono with aprons. I wore a dress and shoes. So I was a city kid with a fancy school bag.

Nonetheless, I was appointed class leader because everyone thought I was the daughter of the assistant manager of the station. No one ever bullied me. When I went home from school, friends would always come and we would go to the ocean together. It was during this year that I learned to swim, which became a favorite activity. Diving and swimming for long distances, I became deeply tanned, and from that time on I stopped catching colds during the winter. After that year when I became a fourth-grader, I entered the Koi elementary school. It was when I went to live in Koi that I started living with my mother and grandmother; my uncle had been promised the post of station master at Hiroshima

Station, but by then Japan was already at war with China. So instead of Hiroshima, he was sent to Shanghai and given the post of station master there.

When the war ended, Japan was flooded with soldiers returning from overseas. My grandmother returned to her farm in Toyoda district. I stayed in Koi with my mother and continued her treatment while working. On the road to Iwakuni, just on the Hiroshima side of the border with Yamaguchi, there is a town called Ōtake. A repatriation reception center was established there, and I started going there to work.

The majority of soldiers who returned after the war's loss came from the south Pacific. All of them were penniless and without means, so they had to be paid as soon as they arrived. From a friend, I learned that the repatriation reception center in Ōtake was looking for people who could do office work. The niece of a lady who taught sewing at her home was a friend of mine, and the two of us went to work at the repatriation reception center together.

The Ōtake repatriation reception center was established a former marine base at Ōtake. The base's barracks and warehouses were used as quarantine stations and for quartering demobilized soldiers. A gate was erected in the front courtyard of the facility, with the words "Thank you for your efforts" on one side, and "Staff of the Ōtake Repatriation Reception Center" on the other. The center opened on December 14, 1945, and by the time it closed on February 21, 1947, it had received over 410,000 returnees from Taiwan, Manchuria, Ogasawara, Okinawa, French Indonesia, Burma, Sumatra, Borneo,

New Guinea, the Solomon Islands and central Pacific. It also returned 1,127 Okinawans to their home.

Dusted from head to toe with DDT as soon as they got off the ship, the soldiers came to us carrying rucksacks and were covered in white. After going through quarantine and before entering their quarters, they were asked to sign and register, and were handed an envelope containing money.

Most of these survivors came ashore carrying rucksacks and canteens slung across their shoulders, but there was one who came before me without either, holding something else in his arms like a great treasure. When he signed the register, I saw that it was Ichirō Fujiyama. He had returned to Japan carrying nothing but his treasured accordion. "Ah! You're Ichirō Fujiyama! We all love you so much. I'm so glad you made it home safely."

Ichirō Fujiyama travelled widely through the south Pacific during the war as a performer with the southern morale and welfare group. He was taken prisoner in Java at the end of the war, and was later transferred to Rempang Island before returning to the Japanese port of Ōtake on an aircraft carrier that served as a repatriation transport.

Located at a former marine billeting facility, the repatriation reception center looked out on a large open area. That evening, in what became something of a welcome home party, Ichirō Fujiyama sang to the returnees while playing the accordion that he carried home. Whether they were remembering the war or their comrades I can't say, but tears flowed freely as the

returnees sang along. And with all the dead and those
who had to be left behind, there was much to remember
and much to cry about.

Also working at the repatriation reception center
was a man named Kiyoshi Takeoka, who was to become
my husband. Kiyoshi lived at Mukainada, and the train
he rode to work in Ōtake was the same one I boarded
at Koi Station on the western side of town. At the
war's end, there weren't many people riding the trains,
and we were always able to sit together and talk. "Why
don't you come and visit me sometime?" he once asked,
and so I went to see him at his house.

When I went to see him, which was about a year
after the bombing, a funny thing happened. I went to
visit him at his home, and when I arrived I happened
to enter the yard through the garden entrance at the
back of the house. There was Kiyoshi, sitting in the yard
wearing nothing but a headband and pair of underpants,
boiling water in a kettle on a charcoal stove. I remember
that when he noticed me, he looked very embarrassed.
I backed out of the rear entrance and went around to
the front, and a moment later he came to greet me after
hurriedly throwing on some clothes. I appreciated the
effort he put into getting properly dressed even in the hot
weather!

"Mother's gone shopping," he said. "I thought
I'd give her some tea when she got back, so I was boiling
water." He was a kind man. And what passed through
my mind, besides having seen him in an embarrassing
condition, was that a person who would go to the trouble
of boiling water for his mother on a hot summer day

might also take good care of my mother.

And that is how I came to know Kiyoshi Takeoka during the year and a half that I worked at the repatriation reception center. All the people in his family were very nice. The eldest brother worked for the Chugoku Electric Power Company, the second brother was a secretary at Japan Steel Works, and they were all very quiet and polite. He had two younger sisters, both of whom were graduates of Shōwa Girls'school, and the household was very harmonious. I had no brothers or sisters, and having been raised as a single child, families with many people were a lot of fun. He was very understanding about my mother's situation, and since he said he would live with us, I decided to marry him.

We rented a house not far from the one where I'd been blown into the yam patch and started our new life as a 3-person family. This was still soon after the war, and finding work was hard. For a while, my new husband helped his father doing contract work for the American military. After marrying, my first baby was a cute little boy who was very white. We named him Hironori. All the neighbors came to see him and took part in our joy. My mother's condition was much improved, and the chaos of the days following the war's end had subsided, so those of us who had lived through that hellish time were starting to see some rays of hope.

But then came January 7, a day when it started snowing early in the morning. Our little Hironori, born so recently, began clenching his hands and legs in suffering. Just a couple of hours earlier, he had been normally breastfeeding, but although he still breathed, his mouth

became stiff and he could not feed. We were deeply distressed, and couldn't understand what the problem might be. With the general lack of fuel for heating, we worried that he might freeze to death. All the ladies in the neighborhood brought wood to burn to help us keep him warm. We thought we'd give him a warm bath and heated up some water, but were stunned when we took off his clothes. From his chest to his tummy, he was covered with the same purple spots that I had had on my arms after the bombing. He died soon thereafter, just 18 days old. The cause of death was "radiation sickness," those sad, sad words. The bomb kept wreaking its woes on us for years and years after the end of the war.

What was once the Koi national school became the Koi elementary school; it was decided to replace the soil in the schoolyard. When it rained, water would puddle in the yard and force cancellation of athletic meets. In some places, the ground was so loose that it would bounce up and down when all the children ran together.

When the soil was replaced, the bones of many people were uncovered. Although over 2,000 people had been cremated in the schoolyard a couple of days after the bombing, some people had been buried without cremation.

When we heard about this, we all got together to help collect the remains for mourning. We picked up the bones, washed them clean with water, wrapped them in newspaper, and then arranged them in the school auditorium. As we arranged the bones, we put those of children in an area separate from the adults.

I remember the mother of one child standing in front of her child's remains in tears. She had come to the

school upon hearing that her child had been found there. She said she had been carrying a photo and searching for her child every day for the three years since losing it to the bomb. She took those tiny bones home with her.

My husband's eldest brother worried about my husband, who had been helping with his father's business. Contracting for the military was fine while the work lasted, but what was he going to do when the flood of work receded? He helped my husband get a position with the Chugoku Electric Power Company.

In those days, it seems that many well-connected people got jobs with Chugoku Electric. All of these people came from good families, but many of them were very fond of alcohol. Most of them did not need their salaries to meet living expenses, and could spend their pay any way they liked. My husband had a boss like that, who invited him to go drinking every night. When we married, he drank very little. He was one of those people who would turn deep red after consuming even a little bit of alcohol.*

When our second son, Seiji, was born, he did not display the bomb sickness symptoms that we worried about. Fortunately, he grew without any problem. Our last child, our daughter Mariko, was also born safely. But by that time, my husband's drinking was becoming a serious problem. You would think that he would refuse such invitations since he couldn't drink much, but he never did; he continued to go along.

---

*Although the practice is in decline, drinking with the boss has long been considered an essential part of getting along in Japanese companies. Those who refuse to drink have been regarded as anti-social.

These sessions always involved heavy drinking, starting with beer, followed by whisky, and finishing with Japanese sake, and my husband would come home reeling.

Since he had a gentle disposition and a kind nature, people started expecting him to pick up the tab. Even when he needed to be home early for some reason, if someone invited him to go drinking, he couldn't bring himself to refuse. All of my husband's good traits were turning against him, and he began sinking lower and lower. It was frightening. In those days, salaries were paid in cash. My husband would take the money and get so drunk that he didn't know what happened to it. Whether he dropped it or had it stolen, when he got home, there would be little money in his pay envelope. This started happening regularly every month.

Then one day a neighbor came to tell me about my husband. She told me that someone was sleeping next to a telephone pole up at the top of the hill, and she thought it was my husband. I was mortified with embarrassment, and when I went to look, there he was, stinking drunk and sleeping with his lunch box as a pillow. It would be bad enough at night, but here he was in broad daylight, drunk in the street instead of doing his job at the company. It made me angry to see my husband in such a pathetic state.

As this continued, my husband became more and more irritable, and started acting violently. Steeped in alcohol, yet unable to accept responsibility for his own actions, he started to turn his anger at himself and against those around him. He began coming home after

50

midnight every night, and we had no money. My mother was suffering from atomic bomb syndrome, and my own constitution was not strong. In addition, I had to take care of two small children. I was completely at my wit's end.

In those days, family members took their baths in a fixed order, starting with the husband of the house and ending with the house's female members. This rule applied even if the husband did not come home until one or two o'clock in the morning. I took it upon myself to feed the children and mother without waiting for my husband's return.* Once, thinking that my husband probably wouldn't come home until two a.m. anyway, I gave my mother a bath first. Unluckily, on that one occasion, my husband came home earlier than usual. When he saw that someone else was using the bath before him, he flew into a rage and dragged her out violently, causing some broken ribs. We had no health insurance at that time, and I could not take my mother to the doctor. So I treated the injury by following directions that my mother, drawing on her experience as a nurse, gave me for wrapping the ribs and applying a compress.

This was not an isolated incident, but part of a pattern of behavior. And so, at 24 years of age, I started thinking about suicide. I thought about it every day, and thoughts about ending my life became a part of it. But I couldn't decide how to kill myself. What if I tried to hang myself and failed? That would be so embarrassing. I thought of throwing myself into the ocean to drown.

* Whether or not to eat before a late-working husband returns home continues to be a topic of concern to Japanese wives down to the present day.

But I had been a strong swimmer since I was a child, and couldn't be sure that I wouldn't lose resolve and just swim back to shore.

I thought about throwing myself in front of a train. Between Koi Station and Yokogawa Station is a place called Yamate-chō. There were radish patches there. It was completely dark at night because at the time it had no streetlights.

There was a hummock there about one meter high that had a lone pine tree at the top. Sometimes, we would hear a train blow its whistle there in the night. When that happened, we'd know that someone had killed themselves near the pine tree. "I heard the train whistle again last night. Looks like another person killed himself." The place was known as a "suicide spot."

It was a cold and snowy winter night. Thinking to jump on the track, I walked to the lone pine tree carrying my baby daughter and holding my 4-year-old son by the hand. The train sounds it whistle on pulling out of Yokogawa Station, so it's easy to keep track of its movement. But at the moment when I started to jump, the baby on my back let out a cry. In that instant, I returned to my senses. Yes, I had intended to take my children with me. My baby's cry jolted me into realization of the wrongness of this. In that instant, my baby Mariko saved our lives.

Now seven years had passed since the bomb. I recalled the coldness of the baby's body that I held to my chest while crouching in that crumpled cistern those many years previously. Again, I felt that rage. I became

filled with loathing at myself for even considering taking the lives of my children along with my own. This was absolutely wrong. It must not be.

Seiji, who I so worried would develop radiation sickness, was now in elementary school. His grades were good, and his teacher asked, "What kind of education are you giving him at home? He seems to be studying hard. Are you having him tutored? I'd really like to know." But I wasn't doing anything. We didn't even have money for full meals, much less tutoring. I wasn't giving Seiji any education at home, and the only response I could give to his teacher's question was one of red-faced embarrassment. There was nothing I could say, because all of the neighbors knew about his father's violence and how he returned home reeling drunk each night.

And then one morning, as my husband was heading to work, I blurted out my feelings.

"I suppose you'll be coming home late again today, but you have children, you know. Would it be too much to come home early once in a while? How am I supposed to bring up our children if life goes on like this? Seiji's teacher wants to know how we're teaching him at home. What am I supposed to tell him? I am sick of this, and I want a divorce."

It all came out at once. I told him I would take the children and find a way to raise them myself. I told him that, with his good job at Chugoku Electric, he would certainly have no problem finding another bride. After all, Chugoku Electric was the top company in Hiroshima; it paid well, distributed bonuses, and had a good retirement

plan. "That's how I feel about this mess. Let's end it."

That day, my husband didn't go to work, but stayed home and started drinking. He knocked back one glass of whisky after another. My mother was out that morning, visiting the city office, and she had taken the baby with her. My husband began rampaging through the house breaking things, and started pulling me around by the hair. He began kicking me, and cutting off my hair; my face puffed up with bruises, which I had all over my body. As he beat me and kicked me, I thought that I didn't care if I died. But as I looked into my husband's eyes, it wasn't rage that I saw, but sorrow; a deep sadness.

Thinking to avoid alerting the neighbors, I had not let out a peep while all this was going on until he started cutting off my hair, and that hurt so much that I screamed involuntarily. The wife of the barber who had a shop directly across the street heard my scream and came running over. When she arrived, she saw clumps of hair scattered about, splatters of blood, and me with my swollen face. "What's going on here?" she cried. "I'm calling the police!"

My husband had a knife in his hand. Maybe it wouldn't have hurt so much if the knife was sharp, but this was an old, rusty knife. At the time, scrap collectors would visit the neighborhood to buy up pieces of scrap metal. I collected pieces of scrap to sell for food money, and this was a knife I had picked up. My husband had been using this to cut off my hair, and the pain was unbearable. That was what broke the limits of my endurance and made me scream.

The day all this happened was during the early

part of the summer school break. Seiji was in his fourth year of elementary school.* He had gone out early that morning to hunt for bugs, and it was this pandemonium that greeted him when he entered the house through the back door after coming home. Seiji came running to me, crying "Mother! You must run away! If you stay here, he'll kill you." And saying this, he pressed a 500-yen note into my hand. How he managed it I don't know, but he told me that a taxi was waiting in front of the house.

I had never given my children any allowance. Perhaps he had saved money given to him when he visited relatives; I don't know. But it was Seiji who put money in my hand and told me to flee for my life.

In that moment, I felt a great calm descending on me. I knew that if I allowed my husband to kill me, it would be my children who would bear the pain throughout their lives. They would have to live life as the children of a killer. And for that reason, I had to run! With that thought, I ran out to the taxi that was waiting in front of the house. I didn't take time to do anything about my appearance, and I'm sure I was a pitiful sight.

The problem was, where could I go? I had no brothers or sisters of my own. My husband's sister had a shop in Shin-Tenchi, and I decided to go there. When she saw me, my sister-in-law was stunned. "Sister! What happened?" She took care of me and washed my wounds. That night, I stayed at my sister-in-law's house. The next day, knowing I had no place else to go, my mother and husband came to get me. This time, it was my fourth-

---

* The Japanese school year begins in April, so the summer break falls in the middle of the school year.

grade son, Seiji, who saved my life.

This was not an isolated incident, but happened several times. Why was this happening to me? Words turned into arguments, which turned into beatings and violence. Alcohol-fueled violence is a fearful thing. I was bruised so much and so often that I couldn't go outdoors. And my husband still came reeling home drunk every night. We had no money. I couldn't help the children with their education. Even though I wanted to divorce, I couldn't. I began truly hoping that my husband would die. That was how much I suffered.

That New Year's Eve, December 31, my husband became involved in a traffic accident. There was a police box near our house, and the policeman stationed there came and told me that my husband was not breathing. He told me to take a blanket for wrapping up the body and to go to the hospital in Itsukaichi. I had no money, so I couldn't go by taxi. My husband's sister had a car and a telephone, and the police called her for me. They came and got me, and we arrived at the hospital just as my husband was coming out of the X-ray room. He hadn't died, but I took no joy in the fact. I had started to lose my humanity. This was just a continuation of that "living hell" in a different form.

3

HOPE

There I was, with my husband the drunk; unhappy together, yet unable to divorce, unhappy with life, yet unable to end it. One unhappy day followed another. Nothing had changed when 1959 rolled around. Unable to ignore my miserable condition, one of the neighborhood wives started visiting regularly. This was Mrs. Yuzuhiro, a tiny lady of enormous good sense who had lost her husband, an elementary school teacher, to the atomic bomb. She was also a member of the Soka Gakkai. Each time she visited, she would read to me from *Nichiren Daishonin - The Novel*, which was being serialized in *Daibyakurenge*, the Soka Gakkai's monthly study magazine.

She urged me to take up the Soka Gakkai's faith, telling me, "Although it is presented as a novel, this story about Nichiren Daishonin is not fiction, but historical fact. I assure you, you'll never feel at a loss again. When you take up this faith, the Gohonzon makes anything possible. If you don't change now, when will you?"

I was no stranger to religion, and I had tried lots of them. But each left me with a sense of some missing truth, and it was that truth which I was seeking. Seeking help in dealing with my situation, I had been to the Tenrikyo, the Risshō Kōsei Kai, and the Kurozumikyō, but couldn't find a sense of conviction in any of them. All of their teachings seemed like fairytales, and nothing in them offered anything that could take root in my heart. I also went to a Christian church that was located near Koi

Station, but their story seemed the most ridiculous of all.

As I listened to Mrs. Yuzuhiro's lucid explanations, I started to develop a conviction that this was the real thing, and a desire to try this faith welled up inside me. When I asked her, "Do you think this is possible for me?" she said, "Absolutely. Changing one's self can make an unhappy person happy, and for someone who is already happy, they can become even happier. That's why it's such a wonderful faith."

As it happened, my mother had already taken up the faith with the Soka Gakkai in 1954, five years earlier at the urging of Mrs. Yuzuhiro, who was about the same age as my mother. Suffering greatly from radiation sickness, my mother practiced diligently with the expressed aim of changing her own life.

Seiji, then in elementary school, asked his grandmother, "Grandma, would it make you happy if I chanted Nam-myoho-renge-kyo?" My mother had told him, "Oh Seiji, that would make me very happy." Whenever Seiji went out or came home, he would go up to my mother's room on the second floor and do Daimoku Sansho. Whenever he received a test from his teacher, or whenever he received a report card, he would go up to the second floor and chant Daimoku. And whenever she went to a *zadankai* meeting, my mother would take the children along with her.

As my children began practicing this faith, my husband was bitterly opposed. Once when my mother held a *zadankai* meeting in her room, my husband actively obstructed it by playing a record at high volume

ın the room immediately below. On another occasion, he yelled at my mother to "get rid of that Gohonzon or whatever you call it before I get home from work." Under the circumstances, I could not start practicing this faith without my husband. If I did, it would just become another subject of arguments, and my husband would be even more isolated. I could not forget the immense sadness in his eyes during the incident when he cut off my hair. My fervent hope was that I could somehow get my husband to start practicing with me.

About this time, my husband started slipping out of the office as soon as he got to work. One day, the company called me in to talk. They told me that my husband was a bad example. In those days, it was very rare for an employee of Chugoku Electric to be fired, but because of my husband's behavior, they wanted him to quit.

"Mr. Takeoka doesn't do any work. He's always disappearing. We usually find him drinking coffee at a nearby coffee shop, or sleeping in the movie theater. The situation is completely impossible. We know that he has two children, and we really hate to do this, but given the situation we have no choice but to ask him to resign."

It was at this moment that I determined that I must start practicing the faith. One of the Soka Gakkai's group leaders was a neighborhood carpenter named Mr. Masui, and I asked him to come to our house. Together we talked to my husband, telling him that we should start practicing.

"What's in it for me?" he asked. "I owe a lot of money at the bar. If I start practicing, will that go away?"

"It will. I am certain of it."

"Then, will it help me stop drinking?"

"It will. Nothing is beyond your reach. If you practice seriously and pray hard, you will find your wish fulfilled."

"Huhhh, and if that doesn't happen, what then?"

"If it doesn't happen, I'll do anything you like."

"My company is about to fire me. Will that go away too?"

"It will. But you've got to make me a promise. Promise you'll do Gongyo every morning and evening, and that you'll do *shakubuku*. You need to practice conscientiously to take strength from the Buddha."

"It would be a big mistake to expect any help from your surroundings, God, Buddha or anything without a willingness to exert effort and change yourself. Living like that would not be true to Buddhism. I'll bet you blame your boss and co-workers for your alcoholism, for luring someone who has no capacity for drink into drinking. That would be a mistake. You should understand that the cause lies within yourself. There are all kinds of temptations swirling around people every day."

Mr. Masui continued talking to my husband with great force and logic. And my husband listened intently, in the end saying, "OK, I'll give it a try." Hearing those words, I felt a great weight lifting from my heart, an incredible lightness. And that day, the two of us joined the Soka Gakkai.

Group leader Masui was a great person. From the very next day, after finishing his own work as a carpenter, he started coming to our house every day

before six to chant Daimoku while waiting for my husband to come home. My husband was a person who kept his promises, and so he came home every day at six and we all did Gongyo together. After Gongyo, my husband went out with Mr. Masui to do *shakubuku*. This went on evening after evening, and my husband started undergoing a profound change. Something was starting to move within him. This happened in November, 1959. It was now 14 years since that August day in 1945.

My husband began bringing home his pay, and drinking less and less. Upon discovering that he was good at paperwork, my husband started getting involved with organizing documents for the Gakkai each day after doing his faith activities. He was still coming home at one and two o'clock in the morning, but while he wasn't getting home any earlier, neither was he coming home reeling drunk. Now he was cheerfully pedaling home on a bicycle.

One day I was called on by Ms. Katsuya, a women's division chapter leader. She was concerned that I was worried by my husband's coming home every day at one and two a.m. She asked me to come to her house that evening at nine. There, she said, I would see what my husband was doing. The person in charge of processing statistical information for the Gakkai on a daily basis was a Mr. Fukushima, who lived in Hakushima. My husband had become an enthusiastic participant in the effort to organize documentation.

"There, you see? The reason he gets home late is that he is wholeheartedly exerting himself on behalf of the Gakkai and all its members. There is nothing for you to worry about."

My husband began enjoying shakubuku activities, and soon thereafter, the two of us were entrusted with roles as group, district, and chapter leaders of the Koi district's men's division and women's division.

At the time, the headquarters of the Soka Gakkai for the Chūgoku region of Japan was located in Okayama. When an executive meeting was held in Hiroshima during a visit of leaders from Okayama, my husband and I participated. On this occasion, the meeting lasted until two o'clock in the morning. Every person attending was asked about the chapter's *shakubuku* activities and goals. The attendees said that they planned to introduce Buddhism to ten or twenty other people, but this only earned them a severe scolding.

"How do you expect Buddhism to save the people of the world with goals of ten or twenty people? Do you think you can achieve *kosen-rufu* like that? What an incredibly stupid thing to say!"

Then he looked at my husband. "You, electrician." Everyone knew that my husband worked at Chugoku Electric, so this was his nickname.

"You, electrician. Can you do better than that? How many people will you convert?"

"Yes! I'll do a hundred people!"

"A hundred? And what will you do if you fail?"

"If I can't do it, I'll shave my head!"

Thereafter, my husband and I, along with the entire chapter, doubled and redoubled our efforts to propagate the truth of Buddhism. Naturally, we recommended our practice to friends and relatives, but we also took our message to beggars living under bridges. It was the

natural thing to do. Having changed our lives and found a way out of a situation that seemed hopeless just three years before, my husband and I told people in all sorts of situations about our faith. As they took up the faith, they changed their lives, found jobs, became leaders in the organization, and even went on to become representatives in the city assembly. As a result of these efforts, 99 new members joined in the Koi chapter.

That was one short. My husband shaved his head. His face was deeply tanned, but the top of his head was white. Looking back, I still laugh to think how funny he looked.

As he exerted himself on behalf of the Gakkai, my husband was also asked to serve as chairman of the labor union at Chugoku Electric. As he set goals for himself in Gakkai activities, he became positive about his work at the company, and started becoming proactively involved in company affairs. Another factor behind this request was his caring nature and natural tendency to take care of people. Now my husband's personality was working to his advantage in many ways.

When my husband asked Gakkai leaders for guidance, they told him, "It's an important position, you should accept it." He also became involved in union activities as well. Including his time as chairman, my husband wound up working for Chugoku Electric for 38 years until his retirement.

As we became involved in Gakkai activities, we started seeing benefits in our family life, and I was able to start doing things I'd always wanted to do. A desire

came welling up within me to undertake activities that would benefit society in general.

I recalled the ambitions I had before entering girls'school. When I began living with my mother and grandmother in Koi, I became very curious about my father and what kind of person he was. This was something I couldn't ask my mother, so I asked my grandmother instead. "Your father is a fine doctor from Okayama. There's nothing for you to worry about. Just study hard, and I'm sure they'll get married eventually." And at that moment, I decided I wanted to become a doctor. I was admitted to the Yamanaka Girls'High School, one of the top two schools in Hiroshima. The school had a history of over a hundred years. It was an august place that had everything, from scholastics to sewing, and it only admitted girls from middle or upper class families. I determined to study there and win admission to Okayama Medical University.

In my second year of girls'school, English was abolished as a subject on the grounds that it was an enemy language. When we went to school, they started sending us out to work all day at uniform or munitions factories. So we all "graduated" without really going through our studies. Later, I was enrolled into the Women's Volunteer Corps and sent to work in a factory that made parts for weapons, so my dream was completely ruined by the war.

My father passed away on December 13, 1964. When we heard about my father's death, my mother and I hurried together to the Doi home in Tadanoumi. Sadly, my mother was not allowed into the house, and had to

wait outside. I alone was allowed to go to my father's bedside. *Shikimi* had been placed in a vase by the bed. Previously, my husband and I came to do *shakubuku* for my father, and through the writings of Nichiren we shared the story of Buddhism. My father promised that he would chant Daimoku. We repeated these visits a couple of times, and I believe the *shikimi* was there at his wish.

Carefully, I lifted the white cloth that covered his face. His expression was very peaceful. His eyes and mouth were half open, and there was a slight smile on his lips. His eyes were looking in my direction, and they sparkled.

"Oh, they're artificial eyes."

My mother, the woman he loved in her youth, also had an artificial eye to replace the one lost to the bomb. Unable to do anything for his daughter and her mother in their time of need, it seemed to me that those eyes were trying to convey a last message. My father had donated both of his eyes to a young student. I thought then that he had fulfilled his duty as a doctor.

Today, my mother and father, and my first son who died just 18 days old, all sleep peacefully in the broad grounds of the Chugoku Memorial Park.

Although I wanted to become a doctor like my father, the turmoil of war prevented me from fulfilling that wish. But I still thought that I'd like to learn a craft worthy of the title "teacher." The first thing I did was strive to become a teacher of knitting. I attended classes at the Fuji Knitting Machine School, and later at the

Brother Company. I took the national examination for knitting, and in April, 1960, one year after taking up the faith with the Soka Gakkai, received notification that I had qualified. Soon thereafter, I opened a knitting school in Koiuemachi and started soliciting students. One of my students was very earnest in her studies and went on to obtain qualification herself. To this day, she runs her own knitting school in Koieumachi.

Around that time, I also submitted an article in a writing contest sponsored by a magazine. Among the various women's magazines published at the time, I was a regular reader of the housewives' magazine, *Shufu-no-tomo*. The magazine carried works of social commentary by well-known feminist authors (such as Chieko Akiyama and Ayako Sono), as well as serializations of novels by well-known writers of historical fiction and political literature, such as Yasushi Inoue, Ineko Sata, and Ryōtarō Shiba. The competition was for works on the theme "Record of Love," which were to be accounts describing love's beauty. The winner would receive a cash prize of 200,000 yen.

On 50 sheets of manuscript paper, I put together an account of our life between when we were married to when we overcame the crisis in our relationship. I entitled it, "Hair in Disarray."

Although I was unable to adequately describe our experience of faith, by this time I had enough emotional freedom to paint a picture in words of that hellish period in our lives. The winners of the competition were announced in the New Year's issue that was published in 1962. Out of more than 600 essays submitted, the works

of three contestants were selected as winners. One of the winners was a piece entitled The Sun Will Not Sink Again by Ritsuko Hayashida of the Asahikawa city in Hokkaido, who is now known as Ayako Miura. Two years later she won renown as the author of *Hyōten* (*Freezing Point*). I was a runner-up, and received a pound of beautiful light blue wool as a prize. This was an amount sufficient to knit sweaters for two adults, and I used it to knit sweaters for my two children. As I knitted, I spent a lot of time thinking about what else I could do with my life.

Seiji enrolled in Shudo Junior High School & Senior High School. There was no leeway in our family finances, so every day-including both summer and winter vacations-he rode his bicycle to school carrying a box lunch. We had no money for a tutor, so we told him to go to the school library and study on his own. We knew that the library was frequented by upper level students, and told him to ask them for help when he had difficulty. He could also obtain help by going to the teachers'room. We told him that he should always learn what he studied during each day, and never to put off learning until the next day.

When Seiji entered his third year of high school, I started running a laundry shop near Koi Station. It happened that one of the Gakkai's group leaders ran a laundry shop. The operation included two outlets, a main shop and a branch. One day, he came to me with a proposition. He said that one of his parents was ill, and he needed a lot of money for medical care and wanted to know if I would buy one of the shops. We were still very

poor, and had to be very careful how we spent every ten yen coin. He wanted me to buy the shop for three million yen. I consulted with one of the senior members at the Gakkai, and he said he thought buying the shop would be a good idea, particularly since the current owner was so considerate of his parent. It wouldn't be necessary for me to do any work, he said, because the current shop employees could carry on operations.

Wondering how we would come up with three million yen, at last I went to my husband's father. Knowing that he wouldn't approve of giving the money to someone else, we told him that Seiji needed money to enter the university. He accepted our request, telling us that we could use the land that his house sat on as collateral to borrow money from the bank.

Using his land as collateral, I borrowed the three million yen from the bank in my own name.

When you borrow three million yen from the bank, you have to leave 500,000 yen in your account, so I withdrew 2.5 million yen, went to the shop owner and handed it to him, telling him to hospitalize his father right away. That very evening, after passing him the money, that group leader and his wife ran away and went into hiding. The title to the shop had not yet been transferred to me. Now I was saddled with a large debt and had no shop.

The barber shop next to the laundry was run by the younger brother of the runaway owner. He was a kind and honest man. When his brother went into hiding, all the employees disappeared from both the main laundry shop and the branch shop next to the barber's. He told

me, "Takeoka-san, I'll make sure my brother takes care of the title. Won't you please take care of the shop?"

Since my husband was an employee at Chugoku Electric, he could not do any other work. With the younger brother's help, I was able to secure title to the shop, but I had none of the skills required to run a laundry.

All this took place while I was serving as a chapter leader in the women's division. I was devoting all my time to Gakkai activities, and had no choice but to trust the shop employees.

After three months, the shop supplier contacted me and said that they had not received payment in many months. The employees had been pocketing the sales revenue and ignoring the bills. Dealing with that was a major headache.

The shop was located close to Koi Station. One summer day I went to the shop and found a man who was clearly a thug standing in front of it. Flashing his tattoos, he said to me, "Are you the one who took over this shop?"

He said that the store was collateral for a loan he had made to the former owner. Therefore, he said, the store belonged to him. Speaking in a loud and abusive manner, his behavior was very intimidating. People were starting to gather around to see what was going on, so I decided to hear him out at my house. Telling him that talking in the street was causing an inconvenience, I shut the shop and headed for home. Taking him to my home in Koiuemachi, I asked him to come in. Entering the house, he saw the *butsudan* in the 8-mat room on the first floor.

"Are you a Gakkai member?" he asked.

When I answered yes, he asked, "What is your position there, ma'am?" When I told him that I was a women's division chapter leader, he placed his hands on the floor and bowed, saying, "Oh, I'm so sorry!" It seems that he was from Osaka, and had been hired by someone who coveted the store. "I am truly sorry! Please go ahead and run the store. I'll make sure that no one like me comes to bother you again." And with that, he left. I was the only one in the house at the time, and inside I was really quite frightened, and so I never got his name. Earlier, I heard that some of the members were doing *shakubuku* to young people in Kyoto and Osaka in an effort to reform them, and I wonder if this young man had been one of the people they talked to.

The situation at the shop was such that I had to let one of the people go, but I couldn't bring myself to give him notice. I chanted Daimoku with all my might about this problem. Then one day a customer came to me, complaining that her clothes had been torn at my laundry. She showed me her coat, which had a rip extending fully one third of the way down the back. When I called the employee and asked if this was his work, he said, "Yes, I did it." I told him, "Since this belongs to the customer, we have to make compensation." And raising his voice he said, "I'm not paying for anything!", and he left the store of his own volition. I felt protected. No matter how ill-behaved, if I'd asked him to quit, I would have had to give him notice, which would have cost money, and he might have felt resentful.

A few days later, the operator of the oldest laundry

shop in the city of Hiroshima came to visit. He was a complete stranger, but had heard that I was having difficulties and came to offer assistance. He was a Gakkai member. At *zadankai* meetings held by the Soka Gakkai, members regularly give encouragement to each other regarding domestic problems, sickness, or problems at work, and I imagine that he heard about some of the things I'd said at meetings.

I told the laundry shop operator how I had come into the store, about my own lack of experience and lack of employees I could rely on. He looked at all the shop's facilities, and said, "Ma'am, all the equipment is just fine. I'll teach you how to use it. Try doing the work yourself. Do good work and this shop can turn a profit for you, then you can pay back your loan. Don't hire anyone, just do the work yourself."

From the next day, this gentleman came to the shop after Gakkai activities and showed me how to do ironing and spot removal, how to wash and hang clothes properly, how to use the equipment, and how to handle clothes made of different materials. The shop had some equipment that, while old, was not commonly found in Hiroshima. I had everything needed to do the work. I realized that the group leader who went into hiding after taking my money had not really meant to cheat me.

With my newly learned skills, I began running the shop by myself, opening it for business early each morning, and then closing it at 7 p.m. before undertaking activities with the Gakkai. I related these experiences to my leaders in the organization, and in return received encouragement and advice. They told me that I should

not neglect the store for activities, and lent support by appointing an assistant women's division leader to take up part of my load. Although there were three other laundry shops nearby, I never lacked customers, and actually had all I could handle.

One of these customers was Kōji Yamamoto of the Hiroshima Carp. He used to park his car in front of the store, and he would request hand washing and ironing when he had to make television appearances. Then there was a noticeable increase in the number of young people coming into the shop. Maybe they found me easy to talk to; they would ask me for advice about many things. With work and talking to young people, I was very busy every day until my seven p.m. closing time.

The person who took the most joy in my taking up the faith and the changes in my husband was my mother.

After the war ended, she became thinner and weaker, and just when I was despairing of her survival, news reached me that the military hospital in Okayama was functioning. I contacted them immediately and had her admitted, and she received treatment at Okayama for a month and a half. The doctors succeeded in keeping her alive. However, the acute symptoms of radiation sickness left her with little strength, and for many years the keloids on the right side of her body pained her whenever winter came. This condition improved slowly over time.

While my mother herself was being treated as an outpatient, people in the neighborhood with minor ailments would come to our house and ask her to look at them. They would come to her for injections as well. In those days, money was still scarce, and people would buy

calcium and vitamins at the hospital and bring them to my mother. My mother would go to the homes of people who couldn't move and look at them there.

Even though she was half bed-ridden herself, she retained a very strong sense of mission from the time she spent as head nurse. I believe that her assistance to other people was one of the things that gave her the strength to live.

Three years after the bombing, her face started itching terribly, right at the base of her nose, and she started scratching uncontrollably. When she'd scratched so much that it started bleeding, out came a small, triangular piece of glass. It was a piece that had been overlooked. My mother's nose was broken in two places at top and bottom, and this piece of glass, which was embedded under the upper break, had taken three years to work its way out.

My mother, who often looked after my children, was the first in our family to take up the faith and chant Daimoku. When my husband was drinking up all his pay, I had no choice but to ask her to look after the children while I did odd jobs to get money for living. During that time, my mother taught my children the importance of chanting Daimoku.

My mother died of stomach cancer on February 28, 1967. Suffering from radiation sickness, she survived for twenty-two years after the bombing. Before she died, Seiji told her that he passed the entrance exam at Chuo University. My mother said, "Help Seiji do what he wants," and died full of happiness.

4

FIGHTING TOGETHER:
FORGING A MISSION FROM MISFORTUNE

Now in my forties, I worked in the laundry every day from early morning until seven in the evening, and didn't have time for indulgences like a leisurely lunch. There was an unending mountain of work. Dressed in old work clothes myself, I sorted item after item according to fabric type, and then laundered and pressed it using a heavy iron to which I added my own weight.

When my daughter Mariko, now a junior high school student at Hijiyama Girls' School, saw my working outfit she cried, "Oh, mama! Do you have to wear that when you're working? Those are awful! If grandma were alive, it would make her cry!" But quitting was out of the question.

On that dark day when I took my children out with the intention of jumping in front of a train, it was baby Mariko's cry that stopped her 24-year-old mother at the brink. When Seiji was in the fourth grade in elementary school, he saved my life from his father. It was also my mother who taught my two children the importance of faith and opened the path for me and my husband to join the Soka Gakkai, making it possible for us to change ourselves, rebuild our lives and know the richness of life. Now we were both working hard to give our children the opportunity to receive a good education.

Soon after my mother's death, Seiji, having passed the Chuo University entrance exam and graduated from Shudo High School, went to Tokyo. All at once, I lost my precious mother who raised me and my son who carried

all our hopes. It was our desire that Seiji enter Hiroshima University and live at home with us, but my mother's last wish was for us to let him do as he pleased.

When Seiji left, I told him, "I am giving you to President Ikeda, so don't feel like you have to return to Hiroshima." But even as I said this, I felt like half of me was being torn away, and experienced a deep sadness. Day after day, I found myself gazing out of the second floor of our Koiuemachi home toward the slope that Seiji climbed on his bicycle when he came home from high school. Seeing this, my husband scolded, "I really wish you would quit that!" But for a year after Seiji's departure, I would catch myself looking out the window of his second floor room down that slope that stretched toward the sea. Keeping busy at the laundry shop helped divert me from such thoughts.

I continued running that shop for over thirty years. I paid back the three million yen after a few years, and the shop was no longer necessary to support our livelihood. Nevertheless, I kept it up to date, replacing old equipment and renovating the interior to maintain a fresh appearance while I kept it running. I hired some help after a while, but kept working myself until I was in my seventies, and then it seemed to become too much of a physical burden.

Just when I was thinking that I would have to quit, Mr. Otsuka, the owner of the building where I rented space for the shop, came to me with a proposal. He said that he needed to replace the structure with a modern building, and paid me a sum of money to vacate the space.

A few years after I started running the laundry, I

was entrusted with the position of chairperson of the Hiroshima chapter of the "Housewives'Alliance," a nationwide housewives'organization. This marked the beginning of fifteen years of activity. It was while I was with the Housewives'Alliance that I began my many years of bearing witness to the atomic bomb.

Chairpersons of the Housewives'Alliance held a biannual national meeting to report on activities at the prefectural level. The first campaign undertaken by the Hiroshima chapter was a thrift campaign, a movement that started in Nagoya. We learned about the Nagoya campaign from the "Housewives'Alliance News," a newsletter published by the Alliance. In Nagoya, the Alliance collected utility bills to learn how much people were paying for utilities. Receipts for water, electricity, and telephone payments were collected and compared, and one family was found to be paying 40,000 yen per month for water. This was an ordinary family of four people, a husband and wife with two children. The household was not being used for business. Most other households were spending around 3,000 yen a month for water, and even those with higher bills weren't paying more than about 5,000 yen. Upon investigation, it was found that the wife was leaving the water running while doing the laundry. Once she quit doing so, their monthly bill dropped to around 3,000 yen.

The theme of our campaign was to take a new look at our life style and make changes to reform it. No matter how rich a society becomes or what conveniences it enjoys, unless housewives are careful about managing their households, society will be weak at its base.

The next thing we studied was milk. I have always liked milk myself, and since I also gave it to the children daily, it was something that had been on my mind.

The milk we were familiar with in my family came from a farm run by a friend, and we regarded it as rich compared to the thin stuff that was sold in town. Enlisting many people to help, we collected samples of all the brands of milk being sold in Hiroshima and compared them for taste. We sorted them according to whether they were rich, thin, or somewhere in between, and then went to the plant where the milk judged the thinnest was produced. When we checked their production methods, we saw things that seemed suspicious. We did not undertake our investigation with the intention of announcing any results; making our finding public would have constituted interference with business. The objective of our campaign was to revolutionize our own lifestyles, so we kept our findings to ourselves, stopped buying milk produced by the company that made the thin product, and only bought from the companies that produced better milk.

At the time, white radishes grown in Hiroshima were selling for about 200 yen apiece. We wanted to know why they were so expensive. Thinking to buy directly from the producers, several of us went to a neighborhood farm with a borrowed small truck. We wanted to buy radishes in bulk for pickling and divide them up between us. When we asked about price, an answer was not immediately forthcoming. As we waited, we wondered why it was so hard to determine a price. The answer we finally received surprised us; it was exactly the same as the retail price.

So we investigated the manner in which these vegetables were distributed. We found that white radishes grown in Hiroshima were transported to Osaka, and then were shipped back to Hiroshima for sale in stores after pricing had been determined in the Osaka market.

For housewives, this was a big problem, so we contacted our representative in the Kōmei party to have them address the issue. We asked that they negotiate with the agricultural cooperative to stop using this intolerable method of pricing the vegetable used most commonly in ordinary households. Soon, the price of white radishes fell, and locally produced radishes were no longer shipped to Osaka and back.

Topics raised by Housewives' Alliance campaigns have subsequently emerged as major social issues. Foreseeing the problems of society's aging population from the late 1970's, we promoted campaigns at the individual level to find responses to these issues as housewives.

The Housewives' Alliance concluded its activities in 1990 after fifteen years of campaigning for smarter living in every prefecture in Japan.

The UN's first Special Session on Disarmament opened in May, 1978, over 30 years after the end of the war. Ahead of the Session, Daisaku Ikeda, the third president of the Soka Gakkai, sent a letter to UN Secretary General Kurt Waldheim listing ten proposals regarding arms reduction and the abolition of nuclear weapons.

On May 20, four days before sending that letter,

President Ikeda opened a leaders' meeting in Hiroshima. Learning that he would be heading to Okayama after leaving the Hiroshima Cultural Center, our family wanted to express our appreciation by seeing him off at Hiroshima Station. Recalling this makes my heart pound even now, and since I can't briefly describe the experience, I'll quote from my diary entry for that day.

> I heard that President Ikeda was visiting the Hiroshima Cultural Center. From early in the morning, I chanted Daimoku for his safe stay in Hiroshima. Mariko and I went to Hiroshima Station with my husband by car. After a while, President Ikeda appeared together with vice presidents Morita, Ueda, and Tokuno. Mariko, Mrs. Itagaki (of the young women's division) and I gazed in President Ikeda's direction. President Ikeda glanced in our direction, took two or three steps in our direction, and said "Thank you for everything. Please take good care of yourselves." We had only come with the intention of seeing President Ikeda safely off from a distance, so we were thrilled at his kind words.
>
> My husband, who had gone out on the platform to see President Ikeda off, was introduced to him by vice president Ueda. President Ikeda told him, "Ah, you're Seiji's father. I know you. Come to Okayama with me. Get on the train with us," and arranged a ticket for him. Mariko and I were in a different location and we couldn't get on the same train, so we headed for the Okayama Cultural Center on the following train.

Taking care of all the arrangements, vice president Ueda told us, "Today, we are all having lunch together. President Ikeda has invited all three of you to join." He escorted us to the large dining room and seated us near the front for a pot dish lunch. President Ikeda said "Good afternoon!" as he came into the dining hall, and then came directly to us, saying, "Mr. Takeoka, I'm so glad you're here." Then he sat down right in front of my husband and did Daimoku Sansho. We were overwhelmed with happiness. I'd never dreamed of such a thing. Filled with a great sense of gratitude for President Ikeda's sincerity and the efforts of all the members at Okayama, we greatly enjoyed that lunch.

All through the meal, President Ikeda extended encouragement and guidance to the individuals who were there. He engaged in practically continuous dialog, tremendously impressing us with his concern for people and showing immeasurable kindness and encouragement.

This experience motivated us to redouble our efforts to contribute to the promulgation of Nichiren Buddhism. Thank you, President Ikeda. May 21, 1978

At the lunch party, President Ikeda spent practically all his time giving encouragement to participants, and had scarcely any opportunity to eat anything himself. Afterwards, he invited the three of us to accompany him to the Shikoku Training Center in Aji, Kagawa.

We then moved from Okayama to the port of Uno, where we boarded a small cruiser for the ride to the

training center. We rode on the same boat as President Ikeda's second son. We reached the training center just before dusk, and as we were enjoying the magnificent twilight view of the Seto inland sea, President Ikeda told my husband, "The sea is beautiful here. Why don't you go for a swim?" When we went to Hiroshima Station that morning, I never could have dreamed how the day would end. Being unprepared for bathing, my husband took his swim in the sea at Aji in his underwear. As he was swimming, President Ikeda came to him in a boat and said, "Ho, Takeoka-san. There are lots of delicious shellfish here. You've got to try the *sazae*." Hearing this, a member who was a fisherman dived into the ocean and collected three or four *sazae* for us.

Even now, over thirty years later, the memories of that day remain fresh in my mind. It was an unforgettable experience for the Takeoka family. My daughter Mariko says, "It was thanks to that day that our family was encouraged to practice faith with pure hearts over the years."

On April 24, 1979, we learned over the radio that President Ikeda had retired as third president of the Soka Gakkai and taken the position of Honorary President. This came as a complete surprise. Why would he retire? It was very unsettling.

The next day, a message of explanation appeared in the *Seikyo Shimbun* under the title "To All Members," but we still couldn't understand or accept this change. We were completely in the dark about what had happened. The 40th Soka Gakkai General Meeting, which

was billed as memorializing the completion of the "Seven Bells," was held at the Soka University Gymnasium in Tokyo's Hachioji on May 3rd. Those who attended the meeting said the atmosphere was gloomy, and there was an unprecedented lack of applause.

For about a year thereafter, President Ikeda disappeared from the pages of the *Seikyo Shimbun*. The disappearance was complete, with not even a line mentioning his name. It was a very sad and lonely year. Our activities, which had been pleasurable and rewarding, became listless and lacking in direction. Throughout the year, we lost confidence that the activities of the Housewives' Alliance and our other activities were reaching the understanding ears of President Ikeda. It seemed to us that there was something missing at the core, and that something important was being overlooked.

It was on April 29, 1980, when President Ikeda returned to Nagasaki Airport from his fifth visit to China, that we finally learned about his activities. The following May 1st, President Ikeda attended a meeting to encourage the youth of Kyushu. Then, on May 3rd, he attended a "Soka Gakkai Day" Gongyo meeting held at the Kansai Culture Center. On the 4th, he attended a chapter leader's meeting in Osaka. Then on the 5th he extended encouragement to elementary, junior, and senior high school students in a "Successors' Day" meeting, followed by young men's and young women's division leaders' meetings and a Kansai friendship meeting.

When President Ikeda started attending meetings again, we learned about the start of a new struggle. We learned that, after that gloomy general meeting a

year earlier, President Ikeda had gone by himself to the Kanagawa Culture Center in Yokohama. There he renewed his determination to adhere to his convictions and resolved to undertake a new struggle to spread the Buddhism of Nichiren Daishonin throughout the world. And there he took up a calligraphy brush and wrote the words 正義 (justice) and 共戦 (shared struggle) as symbols of this determination and resolution.

President Ikeda, our mentor, had returned to us. With joy in our hearts, the members of the Hiroshima Housewives' Alliance took up the new challenge, vowing that they would take up the shared struggle with President Ikeda. Those of us working in Hiroshima vowed to make this our primary mission and strive for its fulfillment. The activity that the Housewives' Alliance of Hiroshima undertook was to interview people and collect their experiences as atomic bomb survivors on tape, and then publish those experiences for posterity.

We first approached about 140 people in various districts, earnestly asking if they would describe their experiences following the bombing in the interests of peace. Every single one of them refused.

None of them wanted it known that they were exposed to the bomb; they were afraid that it would affect the marriage prospects of their sons and daughters. It was just as if they were infected with some communicable disease.

Thirty-five years after the end of the war, the damage inflicted by the atomic bomb was affecting second-generation survivors. There were fears, both factual and otherwise, that the children of parents who

were exposed to radioactivity would produce defective children; they were shunned. Their parents thought that putting such experiences on the record and making them public in a book increase their exposure to such harm. No matter how many people we asked, not one responded positively.

We could understand their feelings. Having lost my own first son to atomic bomb syndrome, and worrying for years afterward about the health of my other two children, I understood all too well. Nonetheless, I thought we had a responsibility to the world's people to leave testimony about the bomb for posterity.

We importuned survivors for three years, patiently asking over three hundred people for cooperation, and finally won agreement from over a hundred. We visited them at their homes, where we had them speak about their experiences and recorded their accounts on tape. Wanting to avoid stiffness and formality, we asked people to speak in Hiroshima dialect and to tell things just as they happened.

Many people asked for assurance that we would not print their addresses. We accurately printed dates of birth and places of exposure, but as promised, we did not include information about where they moved after the bombing. Five years after undertaking this campaign, we finally published our book of recollections in May, 1985. My experience as a survivor is also included. We sent the collection to elementary and junior high schools throughout Hiroshima Prefecture, as well as to the prefectural office, city offices, libraries, and the Peace Memorial Museum.

As chairperson of the Hiroshima Housewives'
Alliance, I wrote the following preface to the volume,
which is entitled "Voices for Posterity – Cries from Hell."

Once, a friend of mine came to Hiroshima and said,
"Forty years after the bombing, with green trees
gracing the streets of Hiroshima and happy-looking
young people wearing the latest fashions wandering
its streets, it is impossible to imagine the misery of
that time, and I wonder whether people's memories
of that day will gradually fade away." At that point,
I cut her off abruptly, saying, "No matter how new
and beautiful the city may look, no matter how
lightly the young folk walk about, the people who
witnessed that instant or lost loved ones to it will
never, ever forget."
     Time and again we visited survivors who did
not want to talk, saying they couldn't remember,
or simply did not want to recall the horror of that
day and the ones that followed. We saw the sorrow
in faces of family members when we went to collect
memories on a promised day, only to be told that
the survivor had been hospitalized with cancer. And
when we learned of survivors who died, there was
regret that we hadn't met them sooner. Having been
exposed myself at the age of seventeen, and having
lost my first son to atomic bomb syndrome soon after
his birth, this was not "somebody else's problem."
In collecting and publishing these recollections, we all
had to overcome such deep sadness.
     The recollections in this book are broadly

grouped according to geographical area. They are reproduced verbatim, and since the witnesses gave their recollections in Hiroshima dialect, in some places they may be hard to understand. We also had to edit some of the testimony because of space restrictions.

All members of the Hiroshima Housewives' Alliance fervently hope that this book contributes in even a small way toward laying the foundation for future world peace.

In closing, I would like to express my heartfelt appreciation to everyone whose cooperation made publication of this collection possible.

Now I would like to express my deep appreciation to the following people who worked so hard on editing that volume:

Keiko Amabe, Mieko Inoue, Kazuko Ueno, Mutsuko Katayama, Ryoko Kitamura, Sumiko Kirihara, Keiko Koide, Kyoko Sakurai, Hiroko Shimoji, Sueko Shinzawa, Sumie Shintani, Mitsue Sente, Chisako Takeoka, Sadako Takeda, Miyako Tatsumi, Kuniko Tazaki, Keiko Nagaoka, Emiko Nishioka, Suzuko Hashiguchi, Reiko Hamaen, Misao Hiraoka, Masako Fukai, Kimiko Furukawa, Masako Masuda, Etsuko Matsuura, Sadae Matsuzaki, Hisako Miyagawa, Akiko Murakami, Fumiko Yamakawa, Emiko Yamanaka

From the time we started collecting recollections until we published our book, two witnesses passed away from cancer. Now another twenty years have passed.

Over half of the hundred and some witnesses, many born in the Meiji and Taishō eras, have now passed away. Even members of the younger cohort, to which I belong, are now in their eighties. Looking back, our project to record testimony of witnesses to the atomic bomb, which we undertook in response to President Ikeda's call for a new struggle, was just about the last opportunity for undertaking such a project.

I think the SGI's many overseas members have sought President Ikeda's guidance just like members in Japan. In 1981, President Ikeda went to the United States for a month in January to give guidance to members. This busy schedule continued when he returned to Japan, as memorial Gongyo meetings were held over a 4-day period in early May at Soka University's central athletic ground as part of the celebration of Soka Gakkai Day. The meetings were bright and joyous affairs that blew away the dark, lingering clouds of a couple of years earlier. We were also invited, and were able to participate in the May 3rd Gongyo meeting and celebratory gathering.

When the Gongyo meeting ended, President Ikeda walked by the place where I was waiting for Seiji near a corridor leading to the university's lecture building next to the gymnasium. I wanted to make myself inconspicuous and avoid rudely intruding, but my body seemed to turn toward President Ikeda of its own accord. Always quick to act, President Ikeda came to me saying, "Ah, you're Seiji's mother, aren't you. I'm so glad you could come. I hope you'll take some time to enjoy Tokyo before returning to Hiroshima." This display of kindness in the

midst of President Ikeda's busy schedule made me feel a warm glow. He offered his hand. I took it in both of mine, and unable to think of anything to say, finally blurted, "President Ikeda! Please fight on and take good care of yourself!" That was all I could muster.

Two days after I returned to Hiroshima, I got a telephone call from Seiji in Tokyo.

"Mom, when you shook President Ikeda's hand, did you say something to him?"

"Everything happened so suddenly, all I could think of was 'Please fight on and take good care of yourself.' Later, I spent a sleepless night thinking that it was very presumptuous of me to tell him 'Please fight on.'"

"I see. Your words gave President Ikeda a boost. He said he was very happy with the encouragement he received from you and from the women's division. I told him that what you wanted to say was that, without his efforts, the Soka Gakkai would crumble."

I felt like I would explode with embarrassment. At the same time, I felt the kindness of President Ikeda's words. "Oh!" I thought, "How could he take time to worry about sucha thing! He must have realized I'd be embarrassed and sent this message with my son to ease my mind!"

A few days later, I learned that President Ikeda had gone abroad to give guidance to overseas members. This was a sixty-one day tour that extended around the northern hemisphere including visits to the Soviet Union, West Germany, Bulgaria, Austria, Italy, France, and the United States. Realizing that he had taken the time to pass this message to Seiji during the midst

of preparations for this trip brought more feelings of gratitude and another long, warm glow. I redoubled my determination to fulfill my own mission.

As work on the compilation of atomic bomb survivor recollections got on track, my wish was fulfilled. In 1982, it was decided we would go to the second United Nations Special Session on Disarmament to be held in New York. Representatives of bomb survivors from Hiroshima and Nagasaki would accompany the Soka Gakkai's delegation, which was participating in its role as a UN-supporting NGO (non-governmental organization). I was one of those representatives.

It was this opportunity to go to the United States and speak directly about the horror I experienced that I had been hoping and praying for ever since holding that poor baby's cold body to my breast 37 years previously.

Captain Robert Lewis, co-pilot of the Enola Gay, the airplane that dropped the bomb on Hiroshima, said that after looking back at the expanding mushroom cloud immediately after dropping the bomb, he wrote in the flight log the words "Oh God, what have we done!" This was on a television program that aired in the United States in 1955. However, I know that Captain Lewis could not even imagine the tragic events that took place under the mushroom cloud on that day. Relating these events was the reason I went to New York.

The UN Special Session on Disarmament got underway on June 7th. Four days earlier, on June 3rd, an exhibition entitled "Nuclear Arms: Threat to Our World" opened at the United Nations headquarters. This was produced by Soka Gakkai youth members from Hiroshima

and Nagasaki. On the 6th, the Gakkai's delegation handed
President Ikeda's "A New Proposal for Disarmament and
the Abolition of Nuclear Weapons" to General Assembly
President Ismat T. Kittani. On the 12th, concurrent with
the Special Session, an anti-nuclear rally was held in
Central Park. About a million people participated in that
rally. A few days earlier, our testimony as atomic bomb
survivors was carried to audiences throughout the United
States by television and radio, as well as in newspapers
such as the New York Times.

That night, many Americans gathered in the hall at
the Roosevelt Hotel to hear us speak. Suppressing my
emotions as much as possible, I spoke about my own
experiences: The horrors I saw as I searched for my
mother, my lost first child, and my fears about the effects
of radiation on my two surviving children. All the time I
talked, I struggled to hold down waves of feeling. Finally
unable to contain myself any more, in closing I made an
emotional plea:

"People of America. I am putting my life on the
line! That's why I've come to New York. I implore you,
please stop making these terrible weapons, and never use
them again. In the interest of world peace, please abolish
nuclear weapons. No other human being must ever again
undergo the experiences that we underwent."

When I finished my testimony, a large man stood up
at the rear of the hall and started walking in my direction.
He came and stood next to where I was sitting, and for
a time said nothing. After a moment, he started crying,
and took my hand, saying, "Mrs. Takeoka. I have done
a terrible thing. When you return to Hiroshima, please

continue your work, and never stop telling people the story you have told today." I squeezed his hand hard. I thought that my fervent plea had lit at least one light for peace in this person's heart. This was what my mission was all about. I prayed with all my might that this light should spread throughout America and all the world.

At the same time, I had a nagging thought: What did he mean by his first words? What did he mean, "I have done a terrible thing"? Did he say "I" because he couldn't bring himself to say "America"? Asking my translator for help, I spent about 5 minutes talking to him. His name was John Montgomery, and he was the Dean for Administration at Harvard University.

After the meeting in which witnesses gave their testimony, we talked to Montgomery, Harvard University professor George Wald (Nobel Prize in Physiology or Medicine), and MIT professor Bernard Feld, who was a participant in the Manhattan Project. They listened intently, trying to grasp the reality of what we had experienced, a reality that could not be conveyed in numerical and scientific data. I imagine they must have had very complex feelings as they spoke directly with people who experienced the bombing first-hand. None of them said very much, but Professor Feld, who was the quietest of all, said at the end, "The tragedy of the atomic bomb must never be repeated in any age. The threat of extinction which these weapons present must be avoided by every possible means."

Later, Professor Montgomery repeatedly visited the Hiroshima Peace Memorial Park and spoke to audiences in the 300-seat lecture hall at the Peace

Memorial Museum. He contributed to the reconstruction of Hiroshima and undertook a variety of other activities on behalf of peace. In 1991, a cherry tree was planted in Professor Montgomery's name outside the Hiroshima Ikeda Peace Memorial Hall to memorialize the efforts on behalf of Hiroshima's reconstruction by Professor and Mrs. Montgomery.

At every one of Professor Montgomery's lectures, I took a seat at the very front of the lecture hall. I didn't want to distract him, so I did not seek him out personally on the first two occasions, but in November 1999, at the end of the third lecture, I approached him, saying "It's been awhile, hasn't it." Professor Montgomery responded in Japanese, saying "Oh, Takeoka-san! You're still alive! I'm so happy. You're still alive! You're still alive!" And then he hugged me. He said he'd been worrying about me ever since we met in New York. I was glad I'd reached out to him again.

Professor Montgomery was an administrative scholar and an expert on urban planning who also served as a soldier from 1942 to 1946. Six months after the bombing, he was sent to Hiroshima at the age of 26 as an advisor to the Hiroshima Reconstruction Planning Commission. During this time, he conducted a detailed survey of the ruined city. He was a very gentle man. But in time of war, soldiers must obey orders. Our real enemy is war, which can transform even the gentlest life into the life of a demon. In condoning the war and serving as a member of the US military, he strongly felt a personal responsibility as a participant in the development of the atomic bomb.

In saying "I have done a terrible thing," Professor

Montgomery proved his sincerity when I met him in New York. In the preface to the Japanese edition of his book, *Aftermath: Tarnished Outcomes of American Foreign Policy,* Montgomery wrote: "I came to these conclusions as a result of my participation in discussions about a freeze on nuclear weapons, discussions that were sponsored by the Soka Gakkai International under the auspices of the United Nations." One and a half years after those discussions, Montgomery met President Ikeda for the first time in January 1984 at the Soka International Friendship Hall in Shibuya. When President Ikeda spoke at Harvard University on September 26, 1991, Professor Montgomery, then a professor emeritus, was the presenter who introduced President Ikeda by summarizing his biography and achievements.

In September 2001, I went to Russia to speak about my atomic bomb experience. During that trip, I visited Volgograd (the former Stalingrad) at the request of the director of the Hiroshima Peace Culture Center. It was a city that concluded a sister city agreement with Hiroshima in 1972. In 1995, Hiroshima and Nagasaki held a joint "Hiroshima-Nagasaki Atomic Bomb Exhibition" in cities of the world's nuclear weapon states. The exhibition was held in Volgograd from September 8th to October 7th.

My husband accompanied me during this mission for peace. We left Tokyo International Airport on September 5th and reached Moscow after a flight of about 10 hours. The trees there were beautiful, their autumn leaves rippling in the chill wind. The next day, my husband and

I boarded an airplane for the trip to Volgograd together with a Nagasaki survivor who came to talk about his experience and the director of the Hiroshima Peace Culture Center. Our mission got underway when we were met by the deputy mayor, the assistant director of Volgograd's State Panoramic Museum, "The Battle of Stalingrad," and interpreters.

Our atomic bomb exhibition was held on the second floor of the museum, which houses a gigantic panorama depicting the fierce battle with the German army during World War II. The Battle of Stalingrad, the greatest urban battle in history, lasted for nine months from June, 1942 to February, 1943. During the battle, the Soviet Union incurred 480,000 military fatalities and another 40,000 civilian deaths, while the German army (including Hungarian, Romanian, and Italian components in addition to the Germans) suffered 400,000 dead. Total casualties from this single battle totaled 1,500,000, a grim toll of lives wasted and disrupted. Once again I was struck by the cruel, disastrous nature of war.

Before visiting Volgograd, I read and re-read President Ikeda's guidance on Russia and the Soviet Union in publications he wrote, such as his "Visit to the Soviet Union."

President Ikeda departed for his first visit to the Soviet Union on September 8, 1974. This was the anniversary of second Soka Gakkai president Josei Toda's declaration condemning nuclear weapons and calling for their abolition. President Toda made his declaration on September 8, 1957 at the "Festival of Youth," a Youth Division Sports Meet held at the

Mitsuzawa Stadium in Yokohama, Kanagawa Prefecture, before an audience filled with 5,000 young members of the Soka Gakkai, saying, "anyone who ventures to use nuclear weapons. . . is a devil incarnate, a fiend, a monster," and calling upon the young people of Japan to spread the intent of the declaration throughout the world.

For me, born and raised in Hiroshima and exposed to the bomb, these words became the precept that gave birth to my determination to forge a mission from my misfortune. Recalling this again now, I reproduce his words in their entirety here.

Today's "Festival of Youth" has been blessed with clear, sunny skies free of any trace of yesterday's storm, as if the heavens themselves have responded to your enthusiasm. With a great feeling of joy, I watched the competitors among you display the Soka Gakkai spirit in each event, as the rest of you wholeheartedly applauded their efforts.

Nevertheless, for all the joy I feel today, it is inevitable that the Soka Gakkai will encounter persecution again. I am also fully prepared to meet any attack that comes my way personally. Having said that, I would now like to share with you what I hope you will regard as the first of my final instructions for the future.

As I have long said, the responsibility for the coming era will be shouldered by the youth. There is no need for me to tell you that *kosen-rufu* is our mission. We must absolutely achieve it. But today I would like to state clearly my feelings and attitude

regarding the testing of nuclear weapons, a topic that is currently being debated heatedly throughout society. I hope that, as my disciples, you will inherit the declaration I am about to make today and, to the best of your ability, spread its intent throughout the world.

Although a movement calling for a ban on the testing of atomic or nuclear weapons has arisen around the world, it is my wish to go further, to attack the problem at its root. I want to expose and rip out the claws that lie hidden in the very depths of such weapons. Thus I advocate that those who venture to use nuclear weapons, irrespective of their nationality or whether their country is victorious or defeated, be sentenced to death without exception.

Why do I say this? Because we, the citizens of the world, have an inviolable right to live. Anyone who tries to jeopardize this right is a devil incarnate, a fiend, a monster. I propose that humankind applies, in every case, the death penalty to anyone responsible for using nuclear weapons, even if that person is on the winning side.

Even if a country should conquer the world through the use of nuclear weapons, the conquerors must be viewed as devils, as evil incarnate. I believe that it is the mission of every member of the youth division in Japan to disseminate this idea throughout the globe.

I shall end by expressing my eager expectation for you to spread this first appeal of mine to the entire world with the powerful spirit you have shown

in today's sports festival.

My mother, who had already taken up the faith at this time, impressed upon me the importance of this declaration by President Toda. She also passed it to her grandchildren.

I learned that I would be conveying my experiences to Russian students on or about September 8th. I spent the days up to my visit to Russia in fervent preparation, carefully reading all of President Ikeda's guidance. Just as in New York, I wanted to forcibly express the view that nuclear weapons are an absolute evil and try to do my part in President Ikeda's battle on behalf of peace.

I spoke about my experience at two national universities in Volgograd. The faces of the young university students, all of the same generation as my grandchildren, brimmed with a shining intelligence, and they listened attentively to my account. After I finished speaking, we had commemorative photos taken together with the students and the deans of the universities.

After each photo session, students gathered around me and started to talk. They encouraged me by saying things like, "Our country, Russia, still has lots of nuclear weapons. After listening to your talk, I am determined that nuclear weapons must never, absolutely never, be used again. We are going to undertake peace activities too. When you get back to Hiroshima, please take good care of yourself and go on working for peace." I keenly felt the importance of continuing to convey my experiences to people of my grandchildren's generation and even younger folk.

In 1989, I became an atomic bomb witness at the Hiroshima Peace Memorial Museum, which gives me the opportunity to speak about my experiences to many people. I have now been serving continually as a witness for over twenty years, beginning with a talk to just a few people at a small city meeting. Those who wish to hear us speak must come to Hiroshima from all over the country. Finding people who are willing and able to serve as witnesses has been a problem. It took several years to reach the current level.

Witnesses often speak to junior and senior high school students, so during the spring and autumn school trip seasons, two halls are often needed to accommodate everyone who comes to listen. Employees of the Osaka city office and their families have made over twenty visits to Hiroshima to hear witnesses speak. The elementary school children in Hiroshima hear me speak of my experiences every year. In the past twenty years, I have spoken over a thousand times, and the number of people who have heard me speak now exceeds 50,000.

At any given time, about thirty people have been continually involved in bearing witness to the atomic bomb over the years, but many witnesses have died, and others have had to stop speaking about their experiences due to age. Up to now, we have been able to keep the program going by enlisting other victims as witnesses.

Since most of the witnesses suffer from the effects of the bomb, they take turns in relating their experiences. My own ability to continue relating my experience for over twenty years comes from my strong sense of mission about working on behalf of peace, which is based

on the teachings of my faith.

My condition always worsens in the summer. In July and August, I feel fatigued and the palms of my hands become hot, even though I have no fever. I have had a doctor examine me, but he could find nothing wrong. He said there must be something wrong with my thyroid gland. I thought I was the only one who suffered from this condition, but when I asked other survivors, I found some who suffered from the same symptoms. This has gone on now for sixty-five years. However, when someone asks me to give testimony, I cannot bring myself to refuse. Because it is my mission, even if I have a bit of a headache or feel poorly, I drink a potion and go out to talk.

When Seiji's son Mitsushiro entered his second year at junior high school, he came to visit me in Hiroshima all by himself during his summer holiday. While showing him around the city, I decided to take advantage of the opportunity to tell him about the war and what my mother and I experienced. It was during that year that our five years of work culminated in publication of our collection of atomic bomb recollections. As in previous years, my palms started getting hot when August arrived.

I told these stories to my grandson over several days as we visited Hiroshima castle in central park, the Japanese garden of Shukkei-en, the atomic bomb dome, and the Peace Memorial Park. I told him about the first son that I lost, the American scientists who developed the atomic bomb, and everything else. He listened intently, and as I took in his serious demeanor, I developed a

conviction: Our hopes and prayers for peace can be transmitted to our children. I renewed my determination to continue down this path for the sake of the children of the future.

As we stood in front of the cenotaph for atomic bomb victims, I told Mitsushiro that ten years previously, President Ikeda had laid a wreath there and chanted Daimoku. I asked Mitsushiro to chant Daimoku with me and pray that all the leaders of the world would come there and pray for peace.

In November, 1975, a day after laying a wreath at the cenotaph, President Ikeda gave an hour-long speech of encouragement to about 10,000 members gathered at the 38th General Meeting of the Soka Gakkai in the Hiroshima Prefectural Stadium. In his opening remarks, President Ikeda said, "I should like to make clear that the decision to hold this meeting in Hiroshima thirty years after the end of World War II reflects our determination to do everything in our power to prevent any recurrence of the nuclear tragedy which destroyed this city and Nagasaki." As one of the 10,000 participants in that meeting, President Ikeda's declaration of determination added new energy to my own personal determination.

President Ikeda went on to speak about the true nature of health and youthfulness saying, "Health cannot be defined merely as the absence of sickness. . . . True health lies in having a sound mind and sound body, with the vigor and capacity to engage in a fully creative life. With such health one can overcome all hardships and can turn even the worst situation into a motivating force to advance." He also extended encouragement to the

members in Hiroshima saying, "The breath of health and youthfulness manifest in the physical and mental sides of an individual's life is not restricted to that person's own human revolution, but works toward healing and revitalization of a sick society and nation." He taught us that making ourselves truly healthy was essential to resuscitating Hiroshima after its devastation by the atomic bomb.

President Ikeda also said, "It is largely owing to the passionate desire for peace which has come from Hiroshima that humankind has not been deceived into using nuclear weapons in any of the wars that have taken place in the last three decades: the Korean war, the Middle East conflict, and the Vietnam War. For this reason, Hiroshima can well be called a holy place, a source of peace to prevent all nuclear war. I insist that, since the Japanese people understand the horrors of nuclear destruction better than anyone else, we have the qualification, the right, and the responsibility to denounce these horrors to people everywhere." I determined that I would change my own life's experience into a mission, and make that mission my life path.

I wrote a letter to President Ikeda, telling him of my joy in being able to convey my atomic bomb experience to my junior high school grandson. To my surprise and delight, President Ikeda took the story about me and Mitsushiro as the basis for a novel entitled "*Trip to Hiroshima*," which was serialized in the Soka Junior High School Culture Newspaper from 1986 to 1987. The novel includes my experience with a junior high school student named "Kazushiro" visiting his aunt "Yaeko," who is an

atomic bomb survivor. Again and again, President Ikeda
has provided us with support and encouragement.

While my grandson and I chanted Daimoku in front
of the cenotaph for atomic bomb victims, I thought
about the greatness of the faith that supported us. My
own earlier life of hopelessness had been completely
transformed, and I came to know the wonder of living.
Now four generations of my family have travelled this
path of faith, starting with my mother Ryō, then me
and my husband, my children Seiji and Mariko, and my
grandchildren Nobuko, Mitsushiro, Emi, and Masayuki.
Now another twenty years have passed. The benefits of
faith that we have received as a family are passing to a
fifth generation. My great granddaughter, Kaori, was born
in March, 2010.

Throughout these four, now five, generations, it has
been President Ikeda and his wife who have provided
the unfailing encouragement that has supported our
faith and the benefits we have accrued from it. When my
mother Ryō read the *Seikyo Shimbun* report of President
Ikeda's appointment as the Soka Gakkai's third
president she said, "This will change the world! This
will be our salvation!" Through our Gakkai activities, my
husband and I were saved from the depths of the hell
that consumed our lives. We learned the joy of living and
found our mission. At each juncture, we received direct,
warm encouragement. It is thanks to this encouragement
from President Ikeda and his wife that I have been able
to carry out my mission. To them, I offer my heartfelt
gratitude. It is impossible to convey the depth of my
feeling in words.

I now know that I was born in Hiroshima and survived the atomic bomb for a purpose. I chose to talk about the misery and cruelty that I suffered in my youth, a subject that many people avoided. But the distress and cruelty wrought by the bomb is something that only those who have survived it can relate. Japan must not be the first country to suffer from this weapon. It must always remain the only country to have been its victim. The experience that this country and the people of Hiroshima and Nagasaki suffered must never be repeated in any country of the world. Atomic weapons must never again be used anywhere on the planet. Conveying this message to my grandchildren, great grandchildren, and to generations beyond is the mission that I learned from President Ikeda, and this is what I have made the mission of my life.

Postscript by Seiji Takeoka

Until I entered elementary school, I was completely bald, without a single hair on my head. I wondered why my head was naked, while other children had lots of black hair. Also, with my sister Mariko, I was one of two children, and for years thought I was my mother's first son, though in reality there was a son born before me.

It was my grandmother who enlightened me about these things. One day, she told me, "Your head is bare because of the *pikadon*" and, "You actually had an older brother who died soon after he was born. It was so pitiful, he turned black all over." That was the first time I heard the word *pikadon*, and I'll never forget the shock that ran through me on hearing that America had dropped this new type of bomb on Japan.

My grandmother, Ryō Kunisada (1903-1967), was the head nurse at an army hospital in Hiroshima. By 8:15 am on August 6, 1945 when the US bomber Enola Gay dropped the atomic bomb on Hiroshima, she had been working continuously at the hospital for several days. At the time of the bombing she was in the Funairi district a short distance to the south of the hypocenter. She lost her left eye to the blast, and her body was pierced in over 200 places by shards of flying glass. Severely injured, for a week she hovered between life and death amongst hundreds of other dead and dying in a school classroom that was pressed into service to hold victims.

At the time, my mother Chisako was 17 years old.

She was serving with the Women's Volunteer Corps. The bomb exploded just as she was about to leave home in Koiuemachi (about 3 kilometers west of the hypocenter) to visit Miyajima with friends, knocking her unconscious and blowing her into a yam patch behind the house. After coming to, she would wander through the ruins of ground zero for days, searching for her mother. I am sure that the horrors this 17-year-old girl witnessed during her search defy description.

Although she escaped injury from the bomb blast itself, her week-long search through the ruins of Hiroshima exposed her to radiation that seriously damaged her lungs, skin, and blood vessels. These were secondary effects of the bomb. Miraculously, she found her mother after a week-long search. Loading her into a cart, she carried her home and there devoted herself to caring for her bedridden mother's bomb-related ailments.

After the war ended, she met a man in the midst of all the chaos, married, and had a child. Just as hope for the future was starting to bloom, tragedy struck again as her beloved son started showing symptoms of atomic bomb syndrome. Black spots rapidly spread across his body, disfiguring it to the point that he no longer looked human. The sadness and pain she felt when the child died despite her efforts to save it are beyond imagination. Still taking care of her bed-ridden mother, she lost her son just as her married life was getting started.

Misfortune followed misfortune, as her husband fell into alcoholism and began exploding into sporadic fits of domestic violence. On December 14, 1948, a second son was born. They named him Seiji. When I was young, I

was called Seibo-kun.* That was my nickname.

I was raised by my grandmother. At bedtime, my parents slept on the first floor, and as soon as my grandmother was able to climb the stairs, I slept with her on the second floor. My earliest memories are of continuous quarreling between my mother and father, and a *butsudan* that at some point appeared in my grandmother's second floor room when she started chanting "Nam-myoho-renge-kyo." When I asked, I learned that she had joined a Nichiren Shōshū lay organization, the Soka Gakkai (which later became independent of Nichiren Shōshū). This was in 1954.

I had heard about the Minobu school of Nichiren, but I thought that my grandmother had gotten caught up in some strange new cult. After a while, my grandmother began hosting *zadankai* meetings on the second floor of our house, and in the evening it became the venue for mini-meetings. Most of the people who came to these meetings were poor or sick, and generally quite pitiful. But, they were all very nice.

One evening, I heard a loud *thud* outside our front door. When I peeked outside, I saw a middle-aged man had collapsed there. When I asked what was wrong, he said that he didn't have bus fare, and so had walked to our house to attend the *zadankai*. He had collapsed from hunger. Grandmother told my mother, "Chii-chan (her nickname for my mother), make this man a rice ball and give it to him to eat." At that, my father exploded, "We

---

* Seibo-kun (誠坊君):*bo* (坊) is a diminutive term of endearment used with male babies and young boys, and *kun* (君) is an honorific used by seniors when addressing (usually male) juniors.

110

don't have rice to feed every stranger that drops in!", and then he turned up the volume of the stereo on the first floor to interfere with the *zadankai*. It went on like that day after day.

Wanting to help my grandmother, and prepared to join a strange religion to do so, I asked her, "Grandma, would it make you happy if I joined?" And she said, "Seibo-kun, nothing could make me happier." That was how I started chanting "Nam-myoho-renge-kyo." Later, my mother and father started practicing, and they both joined the Soka Gakkai on November 7, 1959. On March 5, 1960, I used my spring school break to make a pilgrimage to Taiseki-ji temple at Fuji, where I received the precepts and officially became a member of the Soka Gakkai.

Then one day my grandmother came to us waving the newspaper and crying "wah, wah" as tears poured from her remaining eye. I thought she had gone crazy, and asked "Grandma, what's the matter!" She said, "Now it will be OK! This is good! This is good!" I saw that it was happiness that was overwhelming her, and not grief as I first thought. Getting her to slow down, I found that she was rejoicing about an article in the *Seikyo Shimbun* reporting that Daisaku Ikeda had been appointed as the third president of the Soka Gakkai.

This was just after the death in April, 1958 of Josei Toda, the Soka Gakkai's second president, and the mass media was buzzing with speculation that the Soka Gakkai would disintegrate. My grandmother had introduced many people to the faith, and she was very concerned about what was going to happen.

"Daisuke Ikeda has been appointed as president. No

one will be pointing fingers at the Soka Gakkai now. Now everything will be OK."

I asked her, "Is this Daisaku Ikeda such a great person?"

"Yes, he certainly is," she replied. "Just once, I wish I could meet President Ikeda before I die."

In that instant, I decided to bet my own life on President Ikeda. Even as a child, I recognized that it was faith in the Soka Gakkai that had brought hope to the Takeoka family after its experience with the unsurpassable tragedy of the atomic bomb and its aftermath. From that time on, I started reciting the *Hoben* and *Juryo* chapters of the Lotus Sutra each morning and night; in other words, doing Gongyo.

Soon thereafter, my father and mother were appointed to serve as chapter leaders in the men's and women's divisions, and they became busily engaged in Gakkai activities of all sorts. I started becoming active also, serving in the high school division (a part of today's future division).

One day near the end of 1966, Makoto Hata, one of my teachers at Shudo High School, came to me and said, "Hey, Takeoka! You have a letter!" And he handed a sealed letter to me. The letter was addressed to "Seiji Takeoka, 3rd Year, Shudo High School," and the sender was someone named "Takashi Miyamoto." I'd never heard of him. Wondering what was going on, I opened the letter and read, "I'm writing to you after reading one of your compositions in a youth division collection. When you go to college, I earnestly hope you will take exams at a university in Tokyo. When you do, please contact me at

the following: Takashi Miyamoto, Students'Division Chief, Territory 14."

My father worked at the Chugoku Electric Power Company, and was nothing but an ordinary employee, even if he did serve as a committee head with the All Japan Electric Workers Union. Both my mother and father said, "If you're going to enter college, it has to be a public school. Go to Hiroshima University. That would be OK. We can handle tuition at a public school." So I had no thought of attending college in Tokyo, as they would have to send me monthly living expenses.

Having heard my grandmother say, "Oh, how much I'd like just once to meet President Ikeda," the thought of finding a way to go to Tokyo started taking a fuzzy shape in my mind. But I was in a quandary, unable to broach the subject with my parents, who had worked so hard to raise me.

After New Year's, I summoned up my courage and asked my father, "Look, the private schools hold exams before the public ones. Would it be OK if I went to Tokyo and took the entrance exam for the law department at Chuo University as practice for the public school exam?" And my father said, "Sure, try anything once. Go ahead."

And so, I got on a night train and went to Tokyo. At Tokyo station, I was met by Kan'ichi Nakano, a group leader in the Gakkai's student division. It was at his parents'house in Takadanobaba (his father was Choju Nakano, a parlimentarian in the Shinjuku municipal assembly with the Kōmeitō) that I first met Takashi Miyamoto. Shaking hands, he said, "So you're Seiji! Why not come to the Gakkai's Tokyo headquarters in Tokyo

and work together with us in the student division for *kosen-rufu*?"

I replied, "Sorry, I just came to take the Chuo University entrance exam as a dry run, my first choice is the law department at Hiroshima University. Our family is very poor, and there's no way I can go to school in Tokyo."

His rejoinder was, "Well Seiji, if you do come to Tokyo, I'll arrange for you to see President Ikeda once every month."

I felt a jolt of electricity travel through my entire body. What, I could meet President Ikeda! And not just once, but every month! That evening, I sat in front of the *butsudan* at the Nakano house and prayed with all my might.

"Please, Gohonzon, let me pass the entrance exam for the law department at Chuo University. And please let me come to Tokyo and participate in activities in the student division. Please let me meet President Ikeda once every month. And please give me a compass for my life!"

I prayed with all my might, throwing all the power of my 18 years into my prayer.

The next morning, Mr. Nakano's wife pressed some rice balls into my hand, saying "Take these with you when you go take the exam." In all my life, these thoughtful rice balls were the most unforgettable. I took them with tears of thanks in my eyes, and then went to pour all my strength into the exam.

After the exam, I returned to Hiroshima with a sense of confidence, sure in my heart that I would pass. Now the problem would be convincing my father. When I

left home to take the exam, my grandmother was in the hospital due to her weakening condition. I visited her to tell her about my trip. Even though she was so weak she could not talk, when I told her that I would be able to meet President Ikeda every month if I went to school in Tokyo, she nonetheless clearly told me, "Go!!"

"But Dad is against it," I said.

"Tell him it's my dying wish," she exclaimed.

Notification arrived informing me that I had passed the the law department entrance exam at Chuo University. And then, on February 28, 1967, my grandmother died.

In those days, payment for tuition and enrollment fees at private universities had to be paid before announcement of entrance exam results for public schools. When I told my father, he said, "We really can't afford it, but I can't refuse your grandmother's final wish. But Seibo, if you're going to Tokyo, you had better study with all your might."

Finally the day of my departure for Tokyo arrived. My mother told me, "Seiji, I am sending you to Tokyo so that you can fight together with President Ikeda. Don't feel like you have to return to Hiroshima. Go and join the fight with him." Her eyes brimming with tears, she sent me off.

"Thank you Mother. I'll go and do my best."

Subsequently, I would become a leader in the student division, a vice chief of the young men's division, and a national chairman in the Soka Group (an organization which, at the time, had about 50,000 members and helped ensure safety of members at meetings). Although there

have been many ups and downs along the way, the fact that I have been able to participate without reservation in activities that promote and protect the Gakkai has been thanks to these words of my mother.

Looking back, when Mr. Miyamoto told me that I would be able to meet President Ikeda once a month, he was not far off the mark. I became a member of the monthly leaders'meeting* organizers'staff at the Tokyo headquarters. While I did not speak to him directly, I took great joy in his presence, sometimes inside the hall and sometimes outside.

Then when I served as national chairman of the Soka Group (an organization which, at the time, had about 50,000 members and helped ensure safety of members at meetings), I had the golden experience of being able to speak directly with President Ikeda on an almost daily basis. It was not just that I was meeting him, but that in doing so I was fulfilling my grandmother's order, "Go!", and the spirit of my mother's wish that she was giving me to President Ikeda to take up the fight in his service.

In reading this account of my mother's, I am reminded once again of the depths of her emotions as she let go of her son, who carried all her hopes for the future, while at the same time lost her own mother. I cannot help but feel the great depth of my indebtedness to my parents'generosity.

Their understanding has made it possible for me to put the interests of the Soka Gakkai and the passion of President Ikeda first in my life. Along the way, I have

---

* A regular central activity for the Soka Gakkai which still takes place today.

been protected and supported by many people. This support made it possible for me to overcome a host of problems that seemed insurmountable, bringing me to the point of social and psychological death, and even bringing me face to face with physical death. Even when I had no property or wealth, I always had wonderful friends and comrades.

Taking advantage of this opportunity, I would like to express my appreciation to my father. Currently receiving treatment for a stroke, he is now able to walk again with the help of a cane, and he is fortunately of sound mind. I address these words to him: "Father, who I am today is thanks to you. The many friends I am blessed with are thanks to you. Without discrimination or prejudice to any, you have shown kindness to all. When people needed help, you always extended it without worrying about anyone's opinion. That is the father that I remember as I grew up. Thanks to you, I have been blessed with many friends. Thank you!"

And to my mother I say:

"Mother, thanks to you, when I stood at a fork in life's road, undecided which way to go, you unhesitatingly encouraged me to take the path of setting myself aside and working on behalf of the Soka Gakkai, its members, and its President, Daisaku Ikeda. Despite the difficulties I encountered, it is this that has made my life completely fulfilled. Mother, I, your son Seiji, am determined to continue walking straight along this path."

This account of my mother's, though motivated by a burning desire to convey to posterity the importance of never allowing a repetition of the misery that was

inflicted by the atomic bomb, was also written out of a sense of gratitude to the Soka Gakkai and to President Ikeda for bringing the light of hope to a family that wallowed through a hellish and apparently inescapable quagmire.

The last thing I would like to say is this:

"No matter who you are or where you come from, no matter your age, status, or physical condition, you should promote the Soka Gakkai International's Buddhism with confidence. The Takeoka family of Hiroshima was saved thanks to the lady who introduced Nichiren Buddhism to my grandmother, a petite woman whose severe radiation sickness left her constantly at death's door. It was she who encouraged us in this faith.

On March 16th this year (2010), my granddaughter was born. She is named 'Kaori', a name whose first kanji character is borrowed from the first name of President Ikeda's wife, Kaneko. Now our family's faith spans five generations.

　—My grandmother, Ryō Kunisada

　—My parents, Kiyoshi and Chisako Takeoka

　—My own generation: me, my wife Shigeko, and my sister Mariko and her husband Koji Higashino

　—My daughter, Nobuko Kitabayashi and her husband Daisaku, and my son, Mitsushiro Takeoka

　—My granddaughter, Kaori Kitabayashi

While I am anything but a flower, I will nonetheless say that in taking up this faith, my grandmother was the first of five generations of lotus blossoms including Kiyoshi and Chisako, Seiji and Shigeko, Nobuko, Mitsushiro, and now Kaori.

I sincerely hope that future generations and those who read these words will promote this faith to others with every confidence. I say that the fruit of your efforts to promulgate and educate will plant seeds of faith that will ultimately bloom in the lives of such people like the Oga lotus, which blossomed from a seed that was over two thousand years old.

During the second world war, the faith of Nichiren Daishonin was twisted and perverted by the Nichiren Shoshu school as it pandered to national Shintoism by displaying Shintoistic symbols. One of the few people who resisted this pressure and remained true to the spirit of the true teaching for the peace of the land was first president Tsunesaburo Makiguchi, who died a martyr to his resistance. Another was his disciple, Josei Toda who, standing alone in the wasteland of postwar Japan, said "'Misery' is a word I would like to eradicate from this earth." And then there came Daisaku Ikeda, the Gakkai's third president, who maintained that "Nothing is more barbarous than war. Nothing is more cruel," and asserted that the great human revolution born in the lives of his two predecessors would make it possible to change the destiny of not just a single country, but of all humankind.

With faith in the Sun Lotus.
July 22, 2010, Seiji Takeoka

I would like to express my heartfelt appreciation to my old friend Tokisaku Gomi from my days at Daisanbunmei-sha, Inc. publishing company, who came to Hiroshima three times while bringing this book to publication, and to my schoolmate throughout elementary, junior and senior high school Seiji Yoshinaga, who undertook the book's design.

Postscript to the English edition
by Seiji Takeoka

This book of my mother's, *Hiroshima: Forging a Mission from Misfortune,* was first published at about the same time as I published *Traveler of the Sun Lotus* (December, 2010, a compendium of reflections of my own life's experiences as I head into my golden years).

At my publication party, I gave my mother's book to some close friends along with copies of my own book. The response to my mother's book has been so much greater, and it is now in its third printing.

This edition is our attempt to respond to inquiries from many people who have inquired about the possibility of publishing the book in English.

As a postscript, I would like to add that on January 15, 2013, my daughter Nobuko Kitabayashi and her husband Daisaku—parents of my first granddaughter, Kaori—made me a grandparent yet again with the birth of their son Masaki.

Also, my son Mitsushiro married Kayoko Kikumoto in December, 2011. In July, 2013, he was appointed to leadership positions in the young men's division of the Soka Gakkai and Soka Gakkai International. I am happy to report the birth to them on October 10, 2013 of my third grandchild, Masashiro.

This book describes the experiences of my mother and my grandmother; however, counting from my grandmother, our family now includes five generations

of atomic bomb survivors. To me, this not only proves my family's transformation of the great misfortune of the atomic bomb, but also demonstrates a triumphant revitalization through faith.

In showing the depth of my own gratitude, I am determined to spur myself further onward in growing devotion.

Seiji Takeoka
July 3, 2014, Atago, Tokyo

Note: A Japanese version of this postscript to the English edition will also be included in the fourth Speakman Shoten printing of the Japanese edition.

Glossary

Aioi-bashi (Aioi bridge)   相生橋
An unusual T-shaped bridge in Hiroshima, Japan. The original bridge, constructed in 1932, was the aiming point for the 1945 Hiroshima atom bomb because its shape was easily recognized from the air.

Aji   庵治
Aji was a town located in Kagawa Prefecture, Japan. In 2006, it was merged into the expanded city of Takamatsu and no longer exists as an independent municipality.

Akiyama, Chieko   秋山ちえ子
A female radio personality, essayist, and critic born in Miyagi Prefecture in 1917. As of 2002, she was the host of the world's longest-running radio show, "Akiyama Chieko no Danwa Shitsu" ("Chieko Akiyama's Lounge"), which ran for 45 years from 1957.

butsudan   仏壇
A cabinet that enshrines and protects the Gohonzon, the object of devotion.

Chugoku Memorial Park   中国平和記念墓地公園
A Soka Gakkai memorial park located in the Yamagata district in northern Hiroshima Prefecture.

Chuo University   中央大学
A private university in Tokyo, renowned for its law school. Chuo is one of the most prestigious schools in Japan.

Daibyakurenge   大白蓮華
The Soka Gakkai's monthly study magazine.

Daimoku, Daimoku Sansho   題目
To chant Nam-Myoho-Renge-Kyo. Daimoku Sansho: To chant Nam-Myoho-Renge-Kyo three times.

Danbara   段原
A district in one of the delta areas eastern Hiroshima. Large parts of the Danbara district were shielded from the bomb's blast by Hijiyama, a hill on the eastern side of the city.

Eba   江波
A district in Hiroshima City's Naka ward. Known along with Hijiyama park as one of Hiroshima's best springtime flower viewing places. Over

ten thousand survivors are thought to have taken refuge in Eba after the bombing on August 6, 1945.

Fujiyama, Ichirō　藤山一郎
Ichirō Fujiyama was a singer and composer of Japanese popular music from about 1931 to 1954. He is perhaps best known for his 1949 hit "Aoi Sanmyaku" (Blue Mountain Range).

Funairi　舟入
A district in Hiroshima City's Naka ward.

Gohonzon　ご本尊
The object of devotion. In Nichiren Buddhism, takes the form of a scroll inscribed with Chinese and Sanskrit characters.

Gongyo　勤行
Literally, "assiduous practice." In the practice of Nichiren Buddhism, it means reciting Nam-myoho-renge-kyo, and portions of the Lotus Sutra in front of the Gohonzon. (*See also* Lotus Sutra.)

Hakushima　白島
A district just to the northeast of the Hiroshima castle grounds.

Hesaka　戸坂
A former village in Hiroshima Prefecture's the Aki-gun. Established under the municipality law (町村制) in 1889, it was incorporated into Hiroshima City in 1955.

Hijiyama Girls' School　比治山学園
A private junior and senior high school for girls located in eastern Hiroshima City.

Hiroshima Carp　広島カープ
A professional baseball team in Japan's Central League. Now known as the Hiroshima Toyo Carp, the team was established by Hiroshima Prefecture as part of the reconstruction process from the devastation of the atomic bomb.

Hiroshima Shudo University　広島修道大学
A private university in Hiroshima, Hiroshima Prefecture, Japan.

Human revolution　人間革命
The process in Nichiren Buddhism of bringing about an inner transformation to break through the shackles of "lesser self," bound by self-concern and the ego, and grow in altruism toward a "greater self" capable of caring and taking action for the sake of others. SGI President

Ikeda explains, "There are all sorts of revolutions: political revolutions, economic revolutions, industrial revolutions, scientific revolutions, artistic revolutions…but no matter what one changes, the world will never get any better as long as people themselves…remain selfish and lacking in compassion. In that respect, human revolution is the most fundamental of all revolutions, and at the same time, the most necessary revolution for humankind."

Hyōten　氷点
A book by Ayako Miura. Translated into English as *Freezing Point*.

Inoue, Yasushi　井上靖
Yasushi Inoue was a Japanese writer of poetry, essays, short fiction, and novels from Asahikawa, Hokkaido. He is known for his serious historical fiction of ancient Japan.

Itsukaichi　五日市
A district near the sea on the western edge of Hiroshima City.

Itsukushima Island　厳島
An island in the northwest corner of Hiroshima bay, also popularly known as Miyajima, the "shrine island."

Japan Steel Works　日本精鉱所
A steel manufacturer founded in Hokkaido, Japan in 1907. During World War II, it manufactured the gun barrels for the battleship Yamato.

Kagawa　香川
A prefecture of Japan located on Shikoku island. The capital is Takamatsu.

Kaiten (usu. "Heaven Shaker")　回天
Kaiten were manned torpedoes used by the Imperial Japanese Navy in the final stages of World War II.

kasuri　絣
Fabric that has been woven with fibers dyed to create patterns and images in the fabric.

Koi　己斐
A district in Hiroshima City's Nishi ward, located on the west side of the Ota river floodway. Formerly an independent village, it was incorporated into Hiroshima City in 1929.

Koi-bashi　己斐橋
A bridge located about 2.1 kilometers from the hypocenter. Although

124

partially destroyed by the blast wave, the bridge could still be crossed, and many survivors used to flee from the city to the west.

Koimachi　己斐町
See Koi.

Koiuemachi　己斐上町
A mountainous district in the western part of Hiroshima City.

Kōmeitō, Kōmei party　公明党
Also known as Clean Government Party, the Kōmeitō was a political party in Japan. Before becoming organizationally independent, it was known as the Kōmei Political League, and was a section of the Soka Gakkai. Succeeded by the New Komeito Party.

kosen-rufu　広宣流布
A vision of social peace brought about by the widespread acceptance of core values such as unfailing respect for the dignity of human life.

Kure Naval Arsenal　呉工廠
One of four principal Imperial Japanese Navy shipyards. Over 70% of its buildings and equipment were destroyed by repeated bombing during World War II. Now owned and operated by Ishikawajima Harima, it is one of Japan's few remaining active shipbuilders.

Kurozumikyō　黒住教
Literally, "the teachings of Kurozumi." The religion has Shinto roots, and was founded founded in 1846 by a Shinto priest named Kurozumi, who in 1814 had a Divine union with Amaterasu, Goddess of the sun.

Lotus Sutra　法華経
The Lotus Sūtra is the basis of the T'ien-t'ai (Tiantai) and Nichiren schools of Buddhism. In Nichiren Buddhism, the recitation of the Hoben (Expedient Means) and Juryo (Life Span of the Thus Come One) Chapters of the Lotus Sutra (the "supplementary practice") supports the chanting of Daimoku (the "primary practice").

Meiji　明治
Meiji was the Japanese era which spanned the period from September 1868 through July 1912. Proclaimed after ascension of 14-year-old Prince Mutsuhito to the imperial throne in 1867, the beginning of the era marked the end of the feudal Tokugawa military government. Meiji means "enlightened rule." The frequently chaotic Meiji era was followed by Taishō, which lasted from July 1912 to December 1926.

Minobu school of Nichiren 日蓮宗
The school of Nichiren Buddhism headquartered in Kuon-ji temple at Mt. Minobu in Yamanashi Prefecture.

Miyajima 宮島
Literally, "shrine island" the popular name for the island of Itsukushima, which is located in the northwest of Hiroshima Bay.

Miyajima Station 宮島駅
Now named Miyajima-guchi Station, it is located to the west of Hiroshima on the Honshu mainland opposite the island of Itsukushishima.

Mukainada 向洋
A district located in Hiroshima City's Minami ward.

national school 国民学校
Schools were reformed when the Pacific war started in 1941, and by the National School Order of 1941, elementary schools were redesignated as "national schools" (kokumingakkō). By that order, national schools were to "provide ordinary education in the spirit of the empire and serve the purpose of disciplining the nation at the foundation level."

Nichiren Shōshū 日蓮正宗
A school of Nichiren Buddhism based on the teachings of the 13th-century Japanese monk Nichiren.

Nichiren, Nichiren Daishonin 日蓮
Nichiren was a Buddhist monk who lived in 13th-century Japan. The son of a fisherman, he lived in a time rife with social unrest and natural disasters. His intensive study of the Buddhist sutras convinced him that the Lotus Sutra contained the essence of the Buddha's enlightenment and that it held the key to transforming people's suffering and enabling society to flourish. Based on his study of the sutra, Nichiren established the chanting of Nam-myoho-renge-kyo as a universal practice to enable people to manifest their inherent Buddhahood, gain strength and wisdom to challenge and overcome any adverse circumstances.

Ōhata 大畠
A town located in Yamaguchi Prefecture to the west of Hiroshima. Also Ōbatake (written with the same Japanese characters as Ōhata, but pronounced differently). Merged into the expanded city of Yanai on February 21, 2005.

Okayama 岡山
A city on the Pacific Ocean side of Honshu, Japan's main island,

roughly midway between Hiroshima and Osaka.

Okayama University　岡山大学
A national university in Japan. The main campus is located in Tsushima-Naka, Okayama, Okayama Prefecture. Founded in 1870, it was established as a university in 1949.

Ōtake　大竹
A town in western Hiroshima Prefecture that is situated on the Seto Inland Sea. It was home to important Japanese marine bases during World War II, and after the war was the site of a major repatriation reception center.

pikadon　ピカドン
A Japanese colloquial term for "atomic bomb." *Pika* means brilliant flash, and *don* means boom.

precepts, receiving　御受戒
A ritual acceptance of guidelines enabling practitioners to 'stem wrongdoing and curtail evil.'

repatriation reception center　援護局
An office of the Repatriate Relief Authority (引揚援護院), which was an external bureau of Japan's Ministry of Welfare until its disestablishment on March 31, 1954.

Risshō Kōsei Kai　立正佼成会
An offshoot of the teachings of Nichiren founded in 1938 by Niwano Nikkyō and Naganuma Myōkō. At its outset, Risshō Kōsei Kai was deeply rooted in traditions of folk religion, and shamanistic powers were attributed to Naganuma. Since her death, the group has distanced itself from shamanistic and divinatory practices.

Sata, Ineko　佐多稲子
A feminist author of proletarian literature. Awarded the Noma Prize in 1972 for her book *Juei* (*The Shade of Trees*), which deals with the relationships between Chinese and Japanese people in Nagasaki after the dropping of the atomic bomb.

sazae　サザエ
Turbo cornutus, a species of sea snail, enjoyed as a delicacy in Japan.

Seikyo Shimbun　聖教新聞
The Soka Gakkai's daily newspaper in Japan.

Seven Bells 七つの鐘
A future vision for the Soka Gakkai International conceived by Josei Toda, the Gakkai's second president, who said "Let's sound the bell every seven years to mark our progress toward *kosen-rufu*."

shakubuku 折伏
Assertively expressing the truth of Buddhism to others and challenging views which diminish human life.

Shiba, Ryōtarō 司馬遼太郎
A Japanese author best known for his novels about historical events in Japan and on the Northeast Asian sub-continent, as well as his historical and cultural essays pertaining to Japan and its relationship to the rest of the world.

shikimi シキミ
An Asian evergreen plant, cuttings of which are used in Nichiren Buddhism as an altar offering.

Shima Geka Hospital 島外科病院
Literally, "Shima Hospital of Surgery" Formerly "Shima Hospital," the site of the hospital is considered to be ground zero. The hospital was reconstructed by Dr. Kaoru Shima, who was away from Hiroshima assisting with an operation elsewhere on August 6, 1945.

Shin-Tenchi 新天地
A district in central Hiroshima; known today for "Okonomiyaki Village," and its many *okonomiyaki* (a Japanese dish outwardly resembling a pancake) shops.

Shūdō Junior & Senior High School 修道中学・高校
A boys' school in Hiroshima.

Shufu-no-tomo 主婦の友
Literally, "Housewife's Friend," a magazine for housewives that was published by SHUFUNOTOMO Co., Ltd. from 1917 to 2008.

Soka Gakkai 創価学会
A lay organization based on the teachings of Nichiren Buddhism.

Sono, Ayako 曾野綾子
Ayako Sono is a Catholic Japanese writer of novels, short stories and essays, including *Visitors from Afar* and *Tamayura* ("Transience").

Taishō 大正
See Meiji.

Takadanobaba　高田馬場
An area in Tokyo's Shinjuku ward.

Takajomachi　鷹匠町
The former name of an area in Hiroshima City that is now part of Naka ward.

Takatori　高取
A district in Hiroshima City's Asaminami ward, located on the northern part of Hiroshima City.

Tenrikyo　天理教
A monotheistic religion based on the teachings of a 19th-century Japanese woman named Nakayama Miki. Followers believe that Nakayama is the Shrine of God and God's expression of divine will. The religion's expressed aim is to promote cultivation of Joyous Life through charity and mindfulness.

Toyoda district　豊田郡
A district in Hiroshima Prefecture located on an island in the Inland Sea separating the Japanese islands of Honshū, Shikoku, and Kyūshū.

Uno, port of　宇野港
Uno is a district in Tamano city in Okayama Prefecture that includes the port of Uno.

Women's Volunteer Corps　女子挺身隊
By 1943, depletion of the male population made it necessary for able women to work in factories. The Women's Volunteer Corps was formed, and all women who were "able" (unmarried and old enough to leave school, or about age 15) were required to work. By 1944, the Corps had more than four million women working in industrial sectors such as aircraft manufacturing, munitions, electrical factories, pharmaceuticals, and textiles.

Yamamoto, Kōji　山本浩二
A former baseball player and manager of the Hiroshima Carp. Four times a home run king, he contributed to the team winning five league championships, and was inducted into the Japanese Baseball Hall of Fame in 2008.

Yamanaka Girls' High School　山中高等女学校
A high school for girls located in Hiroshima City's Naka ward. Founded in 1887, it became a national school in April, 1945. The school buildings were destroyed by fire on August 6, 1945.

Yokogawa 横川

Yokogawa is a neighborhood in Hiroshima City's Nishi ward. It is mainly known as a nexus of train travel between Hiroshima City and the northern parts of Hiroshima Prefecture, and between Hiroshima and Japan's San'in region on the opposite side of the island of Honshu.

zadankai 座談会

Discussion meetings in which dialogue is employed to learn how to use religious practice to create happiness in life.

Postscript to the Japanese English Version by Seiji Takeoka

From May 19, 2023 to 21st, G7 Hiroshima Summit will be held by Prime Minister Fumio Kishida. A world leader will meet to the all members to being bombed place Hiroshima, and there is a really significant thing.

This book is 13 years after issuing the first impression in 2010. During this time, my father Kiyoshi died on January 2, 2020. And my mother Chisako which was the author of this book passed away on December 31, the same year.

My son Mitsusiro graduates from Soka Gakkai young man manager. His workplace becomes SGI (Soka Gakkai international) from April, and makes an effort toward world peace and prosperity. In the Higashinos whom my sister married, three great-grandchilds were born. (Yukiha, Hazuma, Akito).

The great-grandchild became seven people in conjunction with the Takeokas. I think that I am certainly pleased with my mother Chisako. They are the fifth generation from my grandmother Ryō Kunisada who they barely come back alive from the dire disaster of the atom bomb, and made existence of the faith.

April 11, 2023, Onna-son Okinawa
Seiji Takeoka